AF594923

UNENGAGED

Building Flourishing Organizations

MATTHEW Q. LESSER

Ballast Books, LLC
www.ballastbooks.com

ISBN: 978-1-955026-85-7

Printed in Hong Kong

Published by Ballast Books
www.ballastbooks.com

For more information, bulk orders, appearances, or speaking requests, please email: info@ballastbooks.com

DEDICATION

To Quentin, Danielle, and Blake. God blessed your mom and me with each of you. You are gifted with talents, minds, and potential to make a difference in the world. Being your dad as you grow, mature, and become the men and woman whom God uniquely created you to be is one of the greatest experiences of my life. Pursue a flourishing life and lead others with empathy, empowerment, and excellence. I admire, adore, and respect each of you, just the way you are. I love you!

TABLE OF CONTENTS

Foreword i

Introduction v

PART I 1

Chapter 1 – The "Un-Formula" Formula . . . 3

Chapter 2 – Meet Paul. 11

Chapter 3 – Engaged Teams. 19

Chapter 4 – Empathy 25

Chapter 5 – Empowerment 37

Chapter 6 – Excellence 53

PART II 63

Chapter 7 – The Flourishing Life Model . . .65

Chapter 8 – Accelerators and Barriers 89

PART III 123

Chapter 9 – Integration: Empathy. 125

Chapter 10 – Integration: Empowerment . . 141

Chapter 11 – Integration: Excellence 155

Closing – Engaged and Flourishing 167

Final Call to Action 177

Epilogue 181

Gratitude 189

Author Bio 193

FOREWORD

We all want to be part of a dynamic culture where our skills are valued, our potential is nurtured, our voice is heard, and our collective efforts produce extraordinary results. In today's world, where toxic work environments seem all too prevalent, it's refreshing to meet and work with leaders who are committed to fostering cultures that attract and retain exceptional talent and serve as a source of inspiration to become the best version of ourselves. *unEngaged* is a valuable guide for leaders like you. It's a compass pointing the way to organizational success by leveraging the power of culture—and elevating it to new levels.

unEngaged is an invitation to join a movement that seeks to redefine the very essence of leadership and organizational health. It's a call to reject the notion that toxicity and disengagement are inevitable and to embrace the potential that lies within each individual and every organization. Matt introduces us to Paul, a leader on a quest to revitalize workplace culture at his friend's company. As we journey alongside him, we gain insights into the foundational pillars found in the best organizations: empathy, empowerment, and excellence. Guided by these principles, Paul navigates through diverse personalities and challenging situations, providing us with valuable lessons that are instrumental to the success of any organization.

This book is a gift to leaders who are ready to embark on a transformative journey toward building a dynamic culture that attracts the brightest minds, drives sustainable growth, and unlocks the full potential of their teams. Matt's dedication and passion for the art of leadership and helping people grow is felt throughout the entire book. He shares practical tools and exercises that leaders from diverse organizations can implement to build healthy, flourishing teams. Whether you are a CEO, an executive, a manager, or an aspiring leader, Matt's unique approach and framework will inspire you to develop and grow in your leadership abilities.

The stories shared throughout the book highlight the incredible transformations that can occur when leaders wholeheartedly embrace the potential of their teams and fully commit to building a remarkable business. Matt reminds us that the path to success lies not only in the implementation of practical strategies but also in the cultivation of a growth mindset—an unwavering belief in the power and potential of people and their ability to shape the destiny of their lives and the organization.

unEngaged encourages us to challenge the status quo, inviting us to transform mediocre cultures into flourishing environments that attract talented people seeking fulfillment and growth. Matt's writing is engaging and accessible, making it easy to absorb the information and envision its application within our own unique context. He has a gift for distilling complex concepts into practical and applicable principles, ensuring every leader—regardless of industry or background—can find wisdom and relevance in his words. Now let's get to work.

Kate Volman
Author and CEO, Floyd Consulting, Inc.
June 2023

INTRODUCTION

Problems seem to follow us, don't they? When we depart home in the morning, we leave one set of problems behind, only to arrive at work and face a new set of problems that have missed us overnight and have eagerly been awaiting our arrival. Problems can be simple or complex; they can be easy to solve or extremely difficult. Some problems can be solved in a matter of seconds, while others take days, weeks, months, or even years to solve.

The most difficult challenges and problems to solve in any organization include attracting quality team members, motivating team member engagement, and inspiring quality team members to be committed for the long term. The same challenges apply in any organization where more than one person is employed, whether business, nonprofits, academia, church, arts, media, athletics, etc. Organizational culture has become a ubiquitous topic and buzzword in modern times. In simple terms, organizational culture can be reduced to one word: people. Organizational culture is all about people.

What kind of organizational culture attracts quality team members, motivates engagement, and keeps quality team members committed for the long term? The answer to this question can be reduced to a simple concept: building flourishing organizations. But how do you do that? The answer is the core focus of this book.

> **What about you? What is the most difficult problem you face right now? What problem is keeping you awake at night? What problem is causing you worry and anxiety?**

Along our journey together, we will pause at specific moments to catch our breath, think about where we are, and reflect. I will guide you during these points with introspective questions titled "What about you?" These questions will help make your journey personal and help you face reality—maybe a reality you have not faced or have not been wanting to face on your own journey. When we stop for these brief respites, I encourage you to keep a journal or keep notes somewhere convenient, so you have a record of your journey. The final leg of our journey will be dedicated to exercises and practical application. Having a record of your thoughts along the way will make it that much more meaningful when we start unpacking how to apply this practically to your life, your leadership, your team, or your organization.

The journey through the pages of this book will wind through stories, examples, and practical solutions that will equip you to build a flourishing organization, regardless of the size and regardless of your position or title. While the primary focus is on leaders and leadership roles in organizations, the concepts, principles, and examples presented herein can be—maybe *should* be—adopted and practiced by anyone, at any time, irrespective of title or position. If you are the owner, CEO, or other member of the executive or senior leadership team in your organization, you have both the opportunity and the responsibility to do whatever it takes to build a flourishing organizational culture where your team members are engaged and committed for the long term. If you are in another leadership or management position, you also have the opportunity and responsibility to build a flourishing organizational culture for the teams and people you lead. If you are not in a leadership position, I encourage and implore you to practice and incorporate the concepts, principles, and examples within to do whatever you are able to do to influence your organizational culture—one person, one team, and one leader at a time.

Before we start our journey of learning how to build flourishing organizations, I want to introduce to you a leader who provided a great example of the importance of intentionally building a culture where team members flourish. Coach Mason's influence transformed a team, families, a school, and a community. I am going to briefly introduce you here and tell the rest of the story at the end of the book.

In 2016, in Butler, Indiana, Eastside High School hired one of its alums, Coach Todd Mason. He had dreamed of one day returning and finishing the journey he had started as the star running back of the Eastside Blazers football team: winning a state championship. When Coach took the reins of the program, the first thing he focused on was the culture. Coach knew that if he did not change the culture, he would have little to no opportunity of leading the team to the state championship. Even though Coach's eyes were set on the championship, his heart's desire was also to raise up men of character and integrity along the way. After struggling mightily for the first three years and only winning a handful of games, the team finally "got it" and embraced what Coach was doing and building. The fourth, fifth, sixth, and seventh years, the team won their divisional sectionals. The sixth year was the magical run that took the team farther than it had ever been, and what an exciting journey for the team, coaches, parents, school, and community.

Coach Mason's story emphasizes this point: culture is critical to the success of the team, both individually and collectively. Regardless of the type of team—business, athletics, or any other team you can imagine—the culture of the team sets the tone for how it will work and function individually and collectively.

There are two basic responses when facing problems in life. The first is to pretend the problem does not exist and either try to run away or hide from it. The reality is that problems rarely just disappear or go away on their own. So, pretending the problem is not really a problem rarely solves things. The second option is to face the problem head-on with courage and with wisdom.

History is filled with women and men who courageously took the reins of their respective organizations and intentionally sought to bring cultural change, sometimes in the face of monumental problems that had huge consequences if not addressed and solved. Many leaders knew the importance of culture: Winston Churchill, Abraham Lincoln, Mother Theresa, Martin Luther King Jr. Each of these men and women faced cultural problems in their lifetimes; many of the problems were complex and multifaceted, with consequences that affected the lives of hundreds, thousands, or even millions. Each of these leaders shared one trait in common: they believed in building a solution bigger than any of them as individuals. They each had to build and mobilize a team that also believed the problem was real and a solution was possible.

Like the aforementioned examples of leaders who faced problems that affected many lives, the focus of this book is on a problem that affects millions, if not billions, of lives around the world every day. The problem is easy to articulate and simple to understand, conceptually, but oh so difficult to solve: how do you create an organizational culture that attracts quality team members, motivates team member engagement, and inspires quality team members to be committed and dedicated for the long term? Over the last few years, the topics of an unengaged workforce and "quiet quitting" have flooded the headlines of newspapers, internet news outlets, and social media. Many researchers and businesses have tried to estimate the economic cost—to their own organizations as well as the economy as a whole—of having unengaged employees as well as a revolving door of employee turnover. Estimates vary widely on what it costs to replace an employee who has departed. Depending upon the position within the organization, cost estimates of turnover range from a relatively small percentage of the position's annual compensation (estimates as low as 20 to 40 percent), to eight to ten times the annual compensation of the position turned over. While the cost of turnover can be quantified more easily for organizations, the cost of having unengaged employees who remain in their positions requires much more speculation. In a study published in February of 2019, Marcella Bremer estimates the following costs of unhealthy organizational culture:

- Toxic Culture = 40 percent, or more, *decrease* in engagement and productivity costing the organization a minimum of $14,000+ (depending upon compensation level of the employee and percentage decrease in engagement) per employee per year
- Unhealthy Culture = 20 percent, or more, *decrease* in engagement and productivity

- Positive Culture = at least 20 percent *increase* in engagement and productivity
- Healthy, Effective Culture = 20 to 30 percent, or greater, *increase* in engagement and productivity[1]

An unhealthy organizational culture raises many questions. Is it possible to get an unengaged employee or team to reengage once they have disengaged? Is it possible to build an organizational culture that creates an individual's desire to "want to" go to work versus "have to"? Is it possible to have a team of people who actively seek to engage and contribute value versus doing as little as possible to "survive" the workday? Is it possible to build an organizational culture that will attract talent? The answer to all of these questions is a resounding YES, but there is always a caveat. The caveat is this: it will not happen by accident or unintentionally. Creating an organizational culture where people not only want to go to work every day but also actively seek to engage and contribute—also known as a flourishing organizational culture—requires two things: desire and intentionality. At its core, unhealthy organizational culture is a simple problem to understand with a solution that requires the desire to fix the problem and the intentional commitment to do something about it.

"Organizational culture" has been a buzz phrase for several years. A simple search will yield thousands of resources at your fingertips. So, why write another book on organizational culture? Additionally, what gives me the authority to address this topic? I spent the first half of my career both building organizational culture and being part of the organizational culture I built. In

---

[1] Bremer, Marcella. "The Cost of a Tough or Toxic Culture." *Marcella Bremer* (blog). February 12, 2019. https://www.positive-culture.com/the-cost-of-a-tough-or-toxic-culture/

the second half of my career, I experienced healthy organizational culture; however, I also experienced dysfunctional and toxic organizational cultures. For many years, I had the privilege of traveling, speaking, and facilitating teams extensively both domestically and internationally. More importantly, I have had the unique and wonderful opportunity to work with hundreds of leaders and the people they lead. I have seen firsthand what happens when teams are part of a healthy, flourishing culture; and I have seen what happens when teams are part of something much less. Teams are people. Organizations are people. Organizations hire people for a job and organizations sell their products and services to…people! *It is all about people*. Always has been. Always will be. When people are part of healthy, flourishing cultures, they can flourish personally and professionally. When people are part of unhealthy, toxic cultures, they do everything they can to survive until another opportunity opens.

My passion for leadership and organizational culture began after I took the reins of my family's business and it started growing rapidly, shortly after it had failed. I had to learn about leadership and organizational culture while in the trenches, doing it every day. I voraciously read books on leadership, and I sought mentors who could teach me practical leadership principles and practices. My passion for leadership and growing healthy, flourishing cultures continues to this day; however, there has been One leader whom I would consider my hero: Jesus. I have spent my life following Him, serving Him, and seeking to understand as much about Him as possible. Jesus was passionate about people. That is why He came. That is why He lived. That is why He died. That is why He rose again. If Jesus was passionate about people (and I know He still is!), I know that I not only should be passionate as well; *I want to be*. When Jesus walked this earth, He met people right where they were, accepted them just as they were, and loved them to help them be better…and He is still doing this today. At its core, this is what leadership is all about: investing in and loving on others to help them be better and help them become the best version of who they can become. Leaders build up, equip, and empower other leaders.

This would be a good place for me to voice a big caveat. My perspective of the world is one where I am a follower of Jesus. I believe Jesus is exactly the person He said He was. From time to time on our journey together, I will mention how my faith in Jesus has influenced and impacted me. I do not do this to proselytize or to push my faith or beliefs on you. Rather, I do this because of the difference Jesus has made in my life. I acknowledge that our culture is becoming increasingly anti-faith, and the mention of the name of Jesus may marginalize me or cause some to deem me to be irrelevant. However, I also believe that there has been much misinformation, poor examples, and intentional gaslighting to skew the name of Jesus from being one of hope and freedom to something sinister and restricting.

I believe in living boldly and living consistently with what one believes to be true. I encourage you to do the same. I do not ask you to believe like I do, and I never will. I respect what you believe, regardless of what you believe. And I only ask for the same respect in return. I have learned much, and I deeply respect many people who do not share my beliefs. We can exist together for mutual benefit and learning without sharing the same belief system. I believe we are all created with an inner sense of wanting to belong to something that is bigger than us, individually. We will do whatever it takes over the course of our lives to fill that "hole" in us to find lasting purpose and satisfaction. My hope and prayer are that you find that deep purpose and satisfaction for your life, and if you ever come to the end of trying to fill that void and find yourself not knowing what to do or where to go next, please contact me. Enough said? I believe in being transparent and authentic, which is why I shared this with you. Now, let's get back to our journey.

Now that the problem is defined, the next logical questions are: "What now? How do we fix the problem?" Great questions! The answer to these questions is the purpose of this book. Throughout this book, we are going on a journey. A journey from "here to there," a journey starting with the basic problem of someone who is unengaged and unmotivated, and finishing with someone who is engaged and motivated. What is the difference? The organizational culture of which he was part. Along the way, we are going to explore both the conceptual and the practical. It is important to discuss and understand the conceptual to have a more complete understanding of the problem and the solution. And it is even more important to understand the practical so you have the "field manual" to implement the solutions we will be discovering on our journey together.

Before we go on, I want to provide you with a map of our journey. This book is laid out like three legs of a journey. The first leg of our journey will unpack the "formula" for the solution to the problem. The second leg of our journey will examine the "Flourishing Life Model," adapted for organizations and organizational life. The final leg of our journey will provide practical tools and exercises to build and sustain a flourishing organizational culture. My hope and prayer for you as we embark together is that this journey will help you, challenge you, and encourage you. I also hope our trip expands your thinking and perspective. Does this sound like a journey worthy of embarking upon? Are you ready to start? I am. So, let's go!

PART ONE

CHAPTER 1

THE "UN-FORMULA" FORMULA

Think back. When were you introduced to your first formula? Perhaps the first formula you can recall is mathematical: 1+1=2. Perhaps the first formula you remember is the secret family recipe to your great-great-grandmother's cinnamon rolls. Oh, those cinnamon rolls! You could smell them as they were baking in the oven. If you close your eyes now, you can smell them again. That sweet aroma filled the house as they baked and you waited, impatiently, for them to come out of the oven. When they were finally finished, waiting for them to cool long enough to frost was like enduring torture. Then, the moment finally came. The rolls had cooled, the frosting was heaped on generously. The first one was cut and carefully removed from the pan—you could see the gooey cinnamon and sugar oozing out of the bottom. You complained because part of your frosting was left behind in the pan and some of the delicious, ooey, gooey cinnamon mess was still left in the bottom of the pan. You wanted every last bite of your roll to be on your plate. Then, the first bite. You took your fork and cut deep into the roll, your mouth salivating. Your heart beating out of your chest as you lifted your fork to your mouth. And then, the moment you had seemingly waited weeks for finally arrived: that first taste. Heaven! Oh my, the collision of flavors—sweet yeast dough, cinnamon, sugar, and cream cheese frosting. You could hardly keep yourself from standing up and singing the "Hallelujah Chorus" as an expression of your inner joy! What an unbelievably pleasant memory.

Wouldn't it be amazing if solving the problems in our lives elicited the same kind of memory as those heavenly cinnamon rolls? Moreover, wouldn't it be even more amazing if solving people "problems" was a simple "formula" that worked every time to provide predictable results? Alas, that is rarely reality. The first leg of our journey is focused on unpacking the "formula" to address and fix the problem of having a culture of unengaged team members. While the solution to the problem is presented as a "formula," I fully admit that I am hesitant to use the word because there is no magic formula to fix the problem of unengaged team members. The "formula" is a simple-to-understand and provocative representation that will help us follow the map of this part of our journey together and provide the framework for the solution. The high-level formula is this:

Engaged Teams = Empathy + Empowerment + Excellence

The balance of the first leg of our journey together will be dedicated to defining and unpacking this formula together. Before we jump into defining components, let's start looking at general definitions of each part.

Engaged Teams. Sometimes it is easier to define what something is by defining what it is not. We will do both in defining "engaged teams," but I think it will be easier for you to understand by starting with the negative before proceeding to the positive. Chances are, you have either been part of or otherwise observed an "unengaged team." You know, the team, or team members, who spend more time and energy figuring out how little they can do instead of just doing what they were supposed to be doing. The team members who spend more time talking about their weekend plans or schedule outside of work than they spend discussing the pressing project due tomorrow. The team members who spend more time *talking about* their colleagues than they do *talking to* their colleagues. Unengaged team members usually are not the root cause of the organizational culture; instead, they are a symptom of the organizational culture. The key to having unengaged team members is often not to replace those team members; some may need to be replaced, absolutely, but a carte blanche, full-on replacement of every team member is rarely the solution. The key is to address the root cause: *the organizational culture*. Having an engaged team is something that grows out of an organizational culture that builds, grows, equips, trains, and empowers engaged team members. Having an engaged team means having engaged team members. An engaged team genuinely cares for one another, implicitly trusts one another, and shares a common commitment to excellence in everything they do together. An engaged team demonstrates empathy for one another. An engaged team is empowered to do the job they were hired to do. An engaged team is all-in and has an unwavering commitment to excellence. That is what an engaged team looks like. That is what an engaged team does.

What about you? When have been part of an engaged team? What did that look like and feel like to you? Have you been part of an unengaged team? What did that look like and feel like to you?

Empathy. At first blush, you may be asking, "What the heck is 'empathy' doing in a definition for building an engaged team and healthy culture?" That is a fair question. It is no mistake that "empathy" is the first characteristic in the formula. Empathy is often downplayed, overlooked, and dismissed as irrelevant—especially in the corporate world; however, time and time again, empathy is emphasized as a key differentiator and competitive advantage in producing engaged and effective teams. Empathy, in its simplest definition, means to care—deeply. Care authentically. Care sincerely. Empathy means putting yourself in someone else's shoes and walking—just as they do. Empathy means getting behind the eyeballs of another person and seeing the world as they do. Sound impossible? Perhaps, but please do not lose hope: it is possible, and I will show you how.

Empowerment. I love the word "empowerment." The word has so many different connotations, meanings, and feelings associated with it in today's culture. My intended use of "empowerment" is its simplest definition: *the granting of the power, right, or authority to perform various acts or duties.*[2] When someone is empowered, they are empowered to do whatever it is they have been asked, or hired, to do. Applying this to the organizational world—small business, large business, nonprofit, church, academia, government, arts, media, or any other organization—empowering someone means giving them the tools, training, knowledge, authority, and accountability to do the job you hired and asked them to do. Period. Too many times, unfortunately, leaders hire people to do a job but then either do not fully equip them to do the job

[2] *Merriam-Webster*, s.v. "empowerment (*n.*)," accessed October 15, 2022, https://www.merriam-webster.com/dictionary/empowerment.

successfully, micromanage them every step of the way, or have unrealistic or unclear expectations of what the job really is. All these lead to one result: *failure*. This is especially true when an organization hires leaders. One of the biggest travesties of leadership is when leaders hire other competent leaders, but then don't let them lead. And then those same leaders wonder what happened—why their "top draft" choice was unsuccessful or did not perform up to their expectations. Simply stated: those competent, proven leaders were never empowered to do the job they were asked to do. Can this failure of leadership be avoided? Can this trend and tendency rampant in today's organizational cultures be reversed? Yes, it can! But it will take unwavering commitment and intentionality. It isn't easy, but I will show you how.

Excellence. Excellence can be difficult to define or explain because it is often in the eye of the beholder. So how do we come to a universal understanding of—and agreement on—what "excellence" really is? Merriam-Webster defines "excellent" as *very good of its kind: eminently good: first class* or *superior.*[3] "Eminently good" is a fantastic way to describe something that is "excellent." Excellence is both a commitment and a result. Excellence is something easily recognizable when it is seen. Excellence stands out from average or good. Excellence is also repeatable. Would you rather be part of a team that is committed to doing something "average," or one that is doing something "excellent"? It is much more rewarding and exciting to be part of something, or part of a team, that is functioning at a high level and consistently produces excellent results than it is to be part of something or a team that produces

[3] *Merriam-Webster*, s.v. "excellent (*adj.*)," accessed October 25, 2022, https://www.merriam-webster.com/dictionary/excellent.

average or mediocre results. Excellence is motivating. The average, full-time worker spends over 2,000 hours every year at work. Considering there are 8,760 hours in a typical 365-day year, that is 23.7 percent of a person's year spent at work. If someone is not motivated or engaged in their work, how many of those 2,000 hours every year are productive hours? As the previously cited study showed, that number is a staggering 40 percent more or less. I do not know many people who enjoy playing on a team that loses day in and day out, who enjoy working in an environment where average or mediocre is the prevailing culture, or who enjoy doing a job where they do not understand how what they do contributes to the mission or vision of the organization or contributes to the greater good. Most people want to be part of something bigger than themselves and be part of something excellent.

> **What about you? When was the last time you were part of something or a team that was committed to excellence? How did that make you feel? How did that motivate you?**

That is the high-level view of the formula. Simple enough to understand, but simple to understand does not translate into simple to apply or implement. In the next few chapters, we are going to unpack the solution we are striving to achieve, engaged teams, as well as unpack each of the components of the "un-formula" formula: empathy, empowerment, and excellence. In the next chapter, we are going to start with the solution, engaged teams, so we understand the destination.

Our journey companion is a middle-aged professional named Paul. We will journey with Paul as he transitions from one company to another. When we first meet Paul, he is part of an organization that has a toxic culture. Paul is tired, exasperated, and at his wit's end. He feels hopeless, to some degree, and is wondering what to do with his life. He is beginning to slip into depression and feels as though his professional career is waning, with little hope of what to do or where to go next.

As we journey with Paul, we will unpack each of the aspects of building engaged, flourishing team members who, in turn, build engaged, flourishing organizational cultures. Along the way, we will also get an inside look at how to apply these concepts to practical constructs and exercises as Paul learns to embrace his new role at Global Solutions, Inc.

Without further ado, it is my pleasure to introduce you to Paul.

CHAPTER 2

MEET PAUL

Paul's first day at his new job finally arrived. He was so excited to get started that he barely slept the night before. A couple of months prior, he submitted his notice at the only job he had known since graduating from college. He had given twenty years of his life to Strategic Concepts, Inc. and Paul thought he would finish his career where he started. Over the course of the previous three years, however, things changed. The culture changed. Honest and open conversations gave way to deception and closed-door conversations. Trusting that your colleagues had your back gave way to perpetually watching your back, so it didn't get stabbed when you weren't looking. Giving and sharing credit gave way to taking others' credit for work well done and blaming when it didn't go well. Praise and affirmation in public, with confrontation and correction in private became reversed: supervisors instead gave praise and affirmation in private, and confrontation and correction in public.

Paul loved his job and loved the culture of the organization. Paul and his teammates would consistently do more than what was asked of them, would actively look for ways to help and contribute, and would voluntarily help and coach the less-experienced members of the team. Paul's team didn't just produce good results; they consistently produced excellent results. But as the culture of the organization changed, so did the performance of Paul's team, other teams, and the overall performance of the organization. Paul noticed that his teammates and other teams began working fewer hours, not offering to help one another—even with looming deadlines that wouldn't be met. What used to take a few days to accomplish was now taking two or even three weeks. Decisions that used to be made at the team level now required sign-off and approval by a minimum of three senior leaders.

Paul began struggling to sleep at night. He started feeling tension in his shoulders, and he began getting terrible headaches. He was eating more and exercising less, causing weight gain. When he arrived home every night, he was exhausted and struggled to interact with his wife and three kids. When he did interact, he was often short and snappy or would miss the conversation because his mind was somewhere else. After four years of watching the culture of the organization he dearly loved spiral from a healthy, high-performing culture where people were actively engaged and excited to come to work every day to a culture where bureaucracy, red tape, and toxicity became the everyday norm of the organization, Paul could no longer take it. He resigned, without having another job to go to.

Six weeks later, one of Paul's roommates from college called. Jude was going to be in town for a few days and wanted to know if Paul could meet for a beer or grab some dinner. It had been years since Paul had seen his old friend. Paul needed some time to decompress and not focus on the job search, but he was also genuinely excited to see his friend. The night of the dinner came, and they met at a local brewpub that had hearty fare and good, cold beer on tap. Paul and Jude spent an hour just catching up on life and enjoying reconnecting. Then, the conversation turned. Jude began talking about his business and the explosive growth he had been experiencing over the past three years. While he was genuinely excited and grateful for the growth, Jude also knew he was going to be in big trouble if he did not bring in experienced, knowledgeable leaders to help him build out the teams necessary to operate a much larger organization while keeping the same commitment to excellence, which was one of their core values as well as their brand reputation. Jude asked Paul to come work with him as one of his key senior leaders to not only build the teams for the organization but also rigorously build and defend the healthy culture of the organization. Paul leaned in. After a couple more hours of discussing the opportunity, and a couple more pints, Paul said that he needed to pray about it and talk with Patty, his wife. On the way out the door, Jude embraced Paul and told him he was excited, genuinely excited, at the thought of being able work with his friend.

As Paul entered his home from the night out with his friend, Patty greeted him at the door. Paul's demeanor was different, much different, than it had been for months! Paul couldn't wait to tell Patty the news. "Patty, Jude offered me a job! He wants me to join his leadership team and head up the people and leadership development for his company. He wants me to start as soon as possible," Paul said. "We would need to move Nashville where the headquarters are located because this kind of role needs to be with the people in the organization. Jude said to take as much time as we need to think and pray about this."

Patty looked at her husband in his near-giddy demeanor, and after several seconds, she responded. "Paul, we have been praying for an opportunity that would utilize your gifts and skills, be something you are passionate doing, something you are called to do, and something you are really good at doing," she said. "From the little I know so far, I think this checks all the boxes, plus one: you get to work with your friend of over twenty years. I am glad that we have a little time to think, talk, and pray; however, I am already seeing a new Paul—my old Paul—and I haven't seen him in a very long time." They embraced and then went to bed. Patty fell asleep as soon as her head hit the pillow. Paul lay awake for several hours, but not because of worry or anxiety; this time it was due to the excitement of working with his friend, whom he genuinely admired, and being part of an organization that was not only doing amazing things in the world but was also a place where the health of the culture and the people were of the utmost importance.

Paul and Patty earnestly prayed and had several discussions over the next couple of weeks, and they came to a decision: Paul would accept the position. Paul called Jude and excitedly accepted. Jude was elated and said he couldn't wait until Paul and his family moved from Fort Wayne, Indiana, to Nashville, Tennessee. Paul and Patty worked as quickly as possible to get their house ready for listing with a real estate agent. Their house was an attractive home with a couple acres of land on the outskirts of town. The housing market was still very strong, and they received three offers within the first twenty-four hours of listing their home. They closed forty-five days later, and thirty days after that, Paul, Patty, and their three kids were on their way to Nashville.

Paul didn't sleep a wink the night before his first day. He was teeming with excitement. Paul got to his new office by 7:00 a.m. ready to get to work. Jude came in around 7:30 a.m. with a big smile and warmly greeted his friend with a huge hug. After a few minutes of catching up, Jude showed Paul to his office. Before exiting, Jude turned around and said, "Paul, I have asked Emma, our Director of HR, to take you through our onboarding process. I know that Emma reports to you now, but I want you to go through this as if you are any other employee on day one. Be fully part of the process and, at the same time, evaluate the process. I want to make sure we have the best processes in the world when it comes to onboarding and developing our people here at Global Solutions, Inc. Do you think you can do this for me?"

Paul responded with an excited "Yes, sir!"

"And that will be the last time you call me 'sir'!" Jude said, laughing as he walked out of Paul's office.

A few minutes past 8:00 a.m., Emma walked into Paul's office and greeted him. "Hi, Paul!"

"You must be Emma," Paul said. "It's so very nice to meet you."

"It's nice to meet you too. Are you ready to jump into your onboarding?" Emma was exactly as Paul had envisioned her by Jude's description. She was in her early sixties, stood five feet ten inches tall, and had salt-and-pepper-colored hair and a warm and welcoming personality that naturally compelled people to sit down, relax, and share about life for a while. Emma reminded Paul of his late grandmother, whom he loved dearly. Paul was lost for a few moments in his thoughts, affectionately recalling the many kitchen-table conversations with his grandmother over fresh, warm cookies right out of the oven and a glass of whole, cold milk.

Suddenly, Paul snapped back into the moment and awkwardly responded, "Yes! I sure am! Let's get this show on the road." By the end of Paul's first day, he was personally introduced to every person in headquarters—all seventy-nine of them. Paul was treated to a very nice lunch with the People and Culture team—his team, or soon to be. While he was meeting the people in the company, the IT team made sure that his computer, desk phone, and mobile phone were connected and working properly. And Paul was shown the critical areas inside the company, like the restrooms, copy room, and the supplies room. By the end of day one, Paul was exhausted and thrilled, all at the same time.

When Paul walked into their newly purchased home that night, the first thing he saw were all the boxes that needed to be unpacked. He had a momentary feeling of being overwhelmed, but that was quickly replaced as Patty, Quentin (oldest son), Danielle (daughter), and Blake (youngest son) came around the corner to greet him. They asked him how his day was, and an unexpected wave of emotion came over him as he barely voiced the words "I am home!" Patty was eager to take Paul to the kitchen. As Paul turned the corner into the kitchen, he saw a lovely bouquet of flowers. "What is that?" Paul inquired.

Patty was eager to share. "Global Solutions sent them today with a lovely note," she said as she read the note aloud. "'We are so thrilled to have you as part of the Global Solutions family!'" Paul choked back the tears that immediately came to his eyes as he smiled lovingly at his wife, who had tears streaming down her cheeks. The rest of that night was filled with conversation, laughter, and joy as Paul and his family shared dinner together and then started tackling the mountains of stacked boxes in their new home. Something was different, Paul thought as he laid his head down on his pillow. But then Patty said what he was thinking as she snuggled up next to him. "It is nice to have you back, my lover!" Then they both drifted off to sleep.

What about you? When did you experience a time when you thought everything was falling apart around you? What did that feel like? And what did it feel like as you came out of that time?

Life. Life is full of highs and lows, mountains and valleys, and victories and failures. The issue is not that we will face these; the issue is how we respond when we face these times. If you react to the lows, the valleys, and the failures with fear, it will only lead to anxiety and a loss of hope. If you respond with patience, courage, and faith that these low times are not the new normal or a systemic shift in your life, you will maintain your strength, your peace, and, most importantly, your hope. Uncertainty and the unknown are part of life; they always have been and always will be. On the flip side, it is equally dangerous to assume that the highs, the mountaintops, and the victories in life will become your new normal. Life has a way of bringing a balance of good and bad, joy and sorrow, and gain and loss. The most important thing to remember during these seasons is that they are not unique, but normal.

> **What about you? What is your response to the natural flows of highs and lows of life? Do you feel fear, anxiety, and a loss of hope in the lows? Do you feel overly confident, exuberant, and invincible in the highs? Either extreme is just that: an extreme. The key is to maintain a balanced and humble perspective when you experience the extremes.**

In the next chapter, we will continue to follow Paul's story as he takes the helm of leadership of his new team in what he thinks is his dream job, in his dream company, leading his dream team.

CHAPTER 3

ENGAGED TEAMS

Paul once again woke up early and was eager to get to work for his second full day. When Paul arrived, he saw an envelope on his desk. He opened it to discover three things. First, a gift card to a local steakhouse with enough money on it to treat his family to a night of fine dining. Second, a stapled grouping of papers that included area churches, area entertainment options, area restaurants, area grocery stores, and other key information helpful for new residents. Third, a letter from Emma outlining the next steps of his onboarding. The letter had several attachments including dates and times for spending half days and full days with each of the teams in the company; dates and times for visiting the company's six other locations; the company's required reading list for all new employees, regardless of position within the company; and a list of key terms, acronyms, and definitions often used by Global Solutions so Paul would feel part of the conversations as quickly as possible inside the company. In addition, Emma had set up a time to meet with their director of training for a full debrief of the assessments Paul completed prior to joining Global Solutions. Paul was overwhelmed, but in a good way. He couldn't wait to dive in.

Over the course of the next six weeks, Paul was able to check all the boxes from the list Emma had given him. In addition, he was working diligently to read the books Global considered critical for culture development and preservation of culture. At the beginning of his seventh week, Jude stuck his head in Paul's office. "You have any lunch plans?" Jude asked.

"No, I sure don't," Paul responded.

"Great! Lunch is on me. Meet me in my office at 11:45 a.m. and we'll ride together to lunch." Paul couldn't wait. He must have checked the clock on his computer every ten minutes or so all morning in anticipation of meeting with his friend and boss. Finally, 11:45 a.m. came and he went to Jude's office. "You ready to go?" Jude asked.

"Sure am!" Paul responded. The two friends walked out of the office and got into Jude's truck to drive to lunch.

At lunch, Jude asked Paul about his first six weeks. Excitedly, Paul recounted the events: meeting everyone at headquarters, traveling to each of the satellite locations, attending meetings, reading books, learning the acronyms and definitions, and even his one-on-one assessment debrief that wound up taking three hours. Jude had a grin on his face as Paul excitedly talked—sometimes so fast that Jude had to interrupt and ask Paul to repeat what he said. Paul talked the entire time while they waited for their food to arrive. When Paul finished, Jude asked one question: "How's your team?"

Paul looked at him, puzzled. "They're good, I guess. I haven't spent a lot of time with them yet because of the onboarding, travel, and learning."

Jude smiled. "I understand. You've been doing exactly what I wanted you to be doing. Now, it's time to take leadership of your team."

Paul looked at Jude with a quizzical look. "Have I done something wrong, Jude?" Paul asked with a little bit of anxiety creeping up in him.

"Absolutely not, Paul! You've been doing exactly what you should've been doing. Now that you've completed your onboarding, it's time for you to lead."

"I understand, boss. I mean Jude. I'm on it!"

They finished their lunch by catching up on one another's families and Paul's settling into life in Nashville. They travelled back to the office in silence, each caught up in his own thoughts.

Paul scheduled a team meeting for midday the next day, telling the team he would have lunch brought in for them. The meeting was scheduled for 11:00 a.m. for three hours, which seemed like a long time for a meeting to last. The time for the meeting came. Paul could hardly wait to meet with his team for the first time as their leader. He started the meeting by asking everyone, individually, to share their story. Paul was specific with his instructions and asked his team not to share the highlights or the "Cliffs-Notes" version, but their story. One by one, the team shared.

By the time Paul's team of seven people had finished sharing, there were only thirty minutes left in the meeting. For the final thirty minutes, Paul asked his team to answer one question: "Why do you work for Global Solutions?" Each team member shared, sometimes with tears streaming down their cheeks, their reasons for working at Global Solutions. After each team member had shared, Paul was a wreck—a good wreck, but nonetheless, a wreck. He sat speechless for what seemed like an eternity, but it was only several seconds before he spoke. "I, ummmm, don't really know what to say. I've been part of a handful of organizations in my life, but none like this. What you shared with me, and with each other, was nothing less than amazing," he said. "I really don't know what to say other than keep doing what you're doing! I'm excited, and humbled, to be part of this team and this organization," Paul continued. "I look forward to the days, weeks, months, and years ahead of us as we work together to make sure that Global Solutions maintains—improves even—the healthy, engaged culture we have. Trust me when I say this: many, if not most, organizations do not have or experience what we have and experience here. We must never take this for granted. We have a huge responsibility to make sure that the culture of this place remains healthy, engaged, and high performing, regardless of how large—or small—we become. This is a huge responsibility, and I am honored—I am humbled—to be on this journey with each of you." Feeling the tightness in his throat and a tear about ready to tumble from his eyes, Paul dismissed the meeting.

When Paul returned to his office, he took a few moments to collect himself, and then he began typing. He typed for the next four hours without a break. He lost all sense of time. The only reason he stopped typing was because he thought his bladder was going to explode! On his way to the restroom, he realized what time it was. He did what he needed to do, went back to his office, finished a few sentences, packed up his stuff, and drove home. What was Paul so engrossed in that afternoon that he lost track of time? He was capturing the "why" of what each of his team members shared earlier that day. Paul wanted to know what it was that made this team, and this company, so special. It seemed like every organization he knew was struggling to fill open positions, keep good team members, and get and keep team members engaged. However, Paul had a team—and was surrounded by a company of teams—that were not only engaged but joyfully so! After Paul captured what his team had shared, he jotted down three words in his effort to put everything into as many manageable "buckets" as possible. Paul's three buckets were: Empathy, Empowerment, and Excellence. These were the last three words Paul typed before he powered down his computer for the day.

Engaged Teams. What does it mean to have an "engaged team"? In a world that struggles with filling open positions, keeping talent, and motivating a workforce that seems nearly impossible to motivate, is it even possible to consider that a different reality exists? Is it even fair to tease with the phrase "engaged team" when it seems like the trend is the sheer opposite of this? The answer is yes, absolutely! What Paul experienced in his first team meeting is not only possible to experience but also possible to build.

> **What about you? Do you lead, or are you part of, an engaged team? If so, what is that like for you? If you do not lead or have not been part of an engaged team, what was that like for you? Remember these differences; we will unpack this in Part III.**

What Paul experienced was unique to him, but it shouldn't be—it should be normal. It should not be unique to be part of something exciting where it seems like everyone is engaged, contributing, and waiting for the opportunity to contribute even more. Imagine what it would be like to be part of something that is exciting, contributes value, and makes a difference in your life and in others' lives. If you want to be part of something like this, you can find it or build it; however, you must be intentional in your search for it, or intentional in how you build it.

Every day, people all over the world wake up and search for something that has meaning, purpose, and lasting value—something bigger than any one person on this planet. And do you know what? Every day, people find what they are searching for! Does it happen the moment you decide to search for it? Not often, but sometimes. Often, it means making two decisions. The first is deciding your current reality is no longer acceptable. Paul made that decision when he decided that working for Strategic Concepts, Inc. was no longer acceptable for his current reality.

> **What about you? Is there anything about your current reality that is not acceptable to you, or no longer acceptable to you? Write down what those issues or circumstances are.**

The second decision is intentionally deciding to do something about changing your current reality to make a new reality. If you are the decision-maker because you are the owner, the CEO, or an influential leader of the company, the decision-making process is quite simple: it is yours to make! If you are a team member of an organization with a toxic culture, like Paul was, it is your decision to make as to whether you stay part of that organization—or not.

> **What about you? Are you the leader of your organization or team? What decisions do you need to make—immediately—to start making changes to your organization's or team's culture? If you are not the leader of your organization, what decisions do you need to make—immediately—to help take your first steps toward a healthier reality?**

In the next chapter, our journey will take us into the first of the three "buckets" that Paul wrote down after his team meeting: Empathy.

CHAPTER 4

EMPATHY

Empathy is a word that is often misunderstood or misused. Empathy is often mistaken for sympathy. When I was growing up, my maternal grandfather, who was one of the most loving, most Godly, and wisest men that I have ever known, shared something about sympathy. He would say, "Matthew! Do you know where you can find 'sympathy' in the dictionary?"

"No," I would answer.

"It is easy," he would say. "You can find it between 'shit' and 'syphilis.' That is where you can find it!" He meant sympathy was for the weak. Period. Unfortunately, because I did not understand the differences between "sympathy" and "empathy," I lumped them both in the same bucket. As a result of that, and compounded with my naturally high-driven, dominant, goal-oriented, task-driven, accomplishment-motivated self, I became neither sympathetic nor empathetic. Prior to a particularly dark time in my life, I was not able to express either sympathy or empathy to anyone—even my spouse. Thankfully, that changed when I was in my late twenties after I went through a deep, clinical depression where I nearly took my own life. I was finally able to put myself into the shoes of another after years of counseling and coaching.

What about you? When you think of "empathy," what words or images come to mind? Does the word "caring" come to mind? How about "understanding?" Or maybe "loving"? Possibly "sharing"? Write down whatever word or words come to mind when you think of "empathy."

Merriam-Webster defines "empathy" as *the action of understanding, being aware of, being sensitive to, and vicariously experiencing the feelings, thoughts, and experience of another of either the past or present without having the feelings, thoughts, and experience fully communicated in an objectively explicit manner.*[4] "Vicariously experiencing" is a tremendous way to define empathy. For me, it took a deep, dark, suicidal depression followed by years of counseling and coaching before I was able to understand, much less express, empathy. My hope and prayer for you is that you can understand and apply empathy in your life well before a dark journey through a deep valley becomes part of your story. Let's return to Paul's story to find out what he learned about empathy in his new role at Global.

The next morning after Paul wrote down the three words—empathy, empowerment, and excellence—he woke up early, eager to get to work. As Paul was getting ready for work, the three words kept bouncing around his head: *empathy, empowerment, excellence*. He nearly forgot to brush his teeth that morning because his mind was so consumed with these words. He poured a cup of coffee in his mobile mug, and then proceeded to leave it sitting on his counter. It wasn't until he was

[4] *Merriam-Webster*, s.v. "empathy (*n.*)," accessed November 15, 2022, https://www.merriam-webster.com/dictionary/empathy.

pulling into the parking lot at work that he realized his coffee was still sitting on the kitchen counter at home. "Oh well," he thought. "I will just have to survive with a crappy cup of coffee at the office today!"

As Paul walked into his office, he noticed that most of the offices were still dark, except for one. Emma was already in her office and was in full motion at work that morning. Paul put his backpack down and then proceeded to Emma's office. Before walking in, he peaked his head around the corner of the doorframe. He noticed she was deep in thought as she stared at her computer screen. He pulled his head back from the door. "Yes, Paul?" Emma inquired. "What can I do for you this fine morning?" Emma asked.

"I'm so sorry, Emma. I didn't mean to disturb you," Paul responded. "I was just checking to see if you were in your office and if you might have a few minutes to chat."

"For you, Paul? Of course we can chat! Come on in," Emma exclaimed excitedly, and she seemed sincere.

Paul proceeded to walk around the corner of Emma's doorframe and sat in front of her desk. He noticed Emma had a look of concern on her face. "Is everything okay, Emma?" Paul asked.

"Ummmmm, sure, everything is fine, Paul," Emma responded hesitantly.

"Ummmmm, I'm not sure I completely believe you, Emma," Paul teased with a grin.

"Well, I don't want to bother you with this, Paul. It's just a normal issue that's common when your job is working with people day in and day out," Emma replied humbly.

"Emma, I know we haven't worked together for very long, but I want you to know that I'm here for you, and I have your back," Paul replied. "I believe in you and support you no matter what you, the team, or any employee is dealing with. So, please share with me what's going on and how I can help."

Emma went on to share that one of the members of the Culture team had just lost a baby after sixteen weeks of pregnancy, and she was devastated. After Emma shared the details and the hurt and loss that their team member was experiencing, Paul slowly responded after a long pause, "I am so very sorry to hear this, Emma. How can we support Jenna during this time? You just shared with me that Jenna and her husband, Carl, have been trying for twelve years to have a baby." Paul paused as he choked back tears. "I don't even know what to say or do right now."

Emma had tears streaming down her face and was trying to keep the sobs from escaping her throat. "Paul, it means the world that you say this. Your predecessor didn't share the same kind of empathy you're expressing right now," Emma said. "I know that Jenna, her husband, and our team are in the right hands at the right time."

Paul looked at her with a confused and inquisitive look. "Emma, this is actually the reason I came down here this morning to talk with you," he said awkwardly. "Yesterday, after our meeting concluded, I went back to my office and I wrote down three words: empathy, empowerment, and excellence. I know we don't have time to talk about all three words today, but I wanted to start talking about the first word today—and hopefully the other two words over time."

"Those three words, Paul…wow! Emma replied after thinking for a moment. "I'm so excited to discuss these with you! I think you've nailed the kind of culture we want to have here at Global Solutions."

Paul sat in silence for a few moments and then replied, “Emma, do you have fifteen minutes so we could discuss the first word, empathy?”

“I sure do!” Emma replied. “This may just be the highlight of my day, and the day is still young.”

Paul and Emma engaged in discussion over the next four hours, completely losing track of time. There was a knock at Emma’s door. “Emma, are you coming to the orientation meeting for the new recruits today?” Andrew asked.

“Of course!” Emma answered, perplexed by the question.

“The meeting started a half hour ago, Emma, and we were just wondering if you were going to make it or not,” Andrew continued.

“A half hour ago! What?” Emma exclaimed. She checked the time on her computer.

“I’m so sorry, Emma!” Paul said. “I completely lost track of time. I would never want you to be late for such an important meeting.”

“It’s fine, Paul. The last four hours were some of the most invigorating I’ve had in a long, long time,” Emma expressed as she gathered her notebook, logged off her computer, and moved closer to the door.

“I look forward to discussing more with you later, Emma,” Paul half-yelled as Emma walked out the door.

As Paul walked out of Emma’s office, he began reflecting on the discussion he had just had for the last four hours; they had covered all three “Es,” not just empathy. When he arrived back in his office, he knew he had about an hour until his next meeting and then he would be slammed with meetings for the rest of the day. For the next hour, Paul typed furiously. He opened his computer, opened a blank document, and wrote one word:

"Empathy." He then began typing everything he could recall from his conversation.

Empathy. What is it? Empathy is the following:

- Empathy is walking a mile in someone else's shoes. *But what does this mean, practically?*
    - Walking a mile in someone else's shoes means considering the other person's perspective as valid as my own. *What? How can that be? How could another person's point of view be as valid as mine?* Considering another person's point of view as valid as my own means taking the time to fully understand why the other person's perspective is valid *to them. To them, that is the key.* Every person has a point of view that is their own, and it is fully valid to them, even if it is not to me—and that is okay! It is not my job, nor my role, to judge another person's perspective as being valid or not. In fact, when I try to do that, I do the opposite of trying to understand that person.

Paul thought and typed at the same time. Lightbulbs were beginning to go off all over the place in Paul's mind as he recalled conversation after conversation he'd had with past teammates, past bosses, his friends, his wife, his kids. Oh, if he could take back the judgmental, hurtful, and flat-out inconsiderate statements he had made over the years.

- Empathy is validating the thoughts and emotions of another person. *Thoughts and emotions? I understand validating another's thoughts, but emotions? Come on.*

- Validating the thoughts and emotions of another person means to acknowledge and express understanding and validation of not only what a person is thinking but also what they are feeling. The key is making sure the other person feels safe and seen, regardless of the intensity of the emotion they are feeling or expressing. Some people are very expressive in their emotions; some are not expressive at all. Either end of that expression spectrum is not only "okay," but it is understood and accepted.
- Validating the thoughts and emotions of another person also means to encourage the person to express their emotions and feelings in whatever way is natural and normal to them. *What? How can that be? I was taught from day one in corporate life that emotions and feelings have no place—none whatsoever—in corporate life. Now I am supposed to throw this all out the window and let other people be all blubbery, let tears flow naturally, or cry openly? What is going on here?*
- *What about my conversation with Emma? If we don't allow people to be who they are naturally, then how can we possibly understand them, build trust with them, and build a relationship with them?* As Emma said, we are playing for the long term here, not the short term. We want the opportunity to speak into the lives of each one of our team members. If we dismiss them or coach them before we understand them, how are we ever going to have the opportunity to speak into their lives?

- Empathy is practicing listening that leads to understanding.
    - *Listening that leads to understanding. I wonder what that really means.*

Paul stood up and walked to the whiteboard in his office. He wrote "Focus" and "Understand" in big letters on the board and connected them with an arrow. Then he wrote "Focus" and "Respond," again in big letters with an arrow connecting them. *So many times, people hear what the other person is saying only long enough to give their response,* Paul thought. *How many times is the inaccurate or inappropriate response given just because I, or the other person, did not take the time to truly understand* before *giving a response? How many relationships have I damaged? How many people have I hurt?* Paul agonized over these thoughts as he continued to pace around his office. After a few minutes of pacing, looking at the board, taking a few steps, stopping, looking at the board again, he mumbled to himself, "These are tied together." He erased the board and then redrew "Focus" with "Understand" below it and "Respond" under that, with arrows connecting them together in a downward fashion. "Focus—Understand—Respond," Paul muttered. "Empathy is more than just understanding. There is something missing," Paul whispered to himself.

He went back to his computer and reread what he had written. Then, he read his handwritten notes from his meeting with Emma. He spent some time looking up words in the online dictionary and thesaurus, trying to come up with some idea of what was missing—something to give more emphasis to understanding. He came across the word "considerate" and thought, *This is a good word. Being empathetic is being considerate…but that is a noun and I need a verb.* He thought for a minute. *Considering is not strong enough. To truly understand, I must* accept *what the other person is saying, even if I do not agree; accepting has nothing to do with agreement.* He walked over to his whiteboard, erased it, and started again. "Focus." "Understand." "Accept." "Respond." He stepped back from the board after he wrote those four words with arrows connecting them. "All verbs. All one word," Paul muttered to himself. A smile came to his face. "I think this properly links listening and empathy together. I like it!" Paul whispered.

After finishing typing up his notes on empathy from his morning discussion with Emma, Paul closed his laptop and went about the rest of his day. He knew he still had to type up his notes from their discussion on empowerment and excellence, but he was satisfied with his progress for now.

Empathy. In recent years, the word "empathy" has become a common nomenclature in discussions related to organizational health. Even though discussions around empathy have become more common and accepted by organizational leadership, it is still widely misunderstood. Not understanding is the fundamental problem. Without understanding empathy, little to no agreement can occur on how to practice or integrate empathy into organizational culture. Until recent times, empathy was not only not in the discussion, but it was also often unwanted. The perception of empathy was that of weakness, softness, and unwelcome emotion. Organizations thought if they allowed empathy in, productivity would decrease exponentially. As happens in every culture, time brings change and evolution of norms and mores. Organizational culture is no exception. The world went through universal upheaval during the COVID-19 pandemic. At the same time, younger generations were taking more prominent roles in organizational life and leadership, and social and political unrest increased around the world. All of these served as catalysts for fundamental shifts in thinking, especially to the worlds of human resources, people development, and leadership development.

People comprise organizations. Organizations employ people who sell to or otherwise serve customers—who are also *people.* It is too easy when looking at financial statements and annual reports to see the facts and figures but forget that they represent one common feature: *people.* Whenever the terms "FTE" or "human resource" are used, it means one thing and one thing only: *people.* People with spouses and kids. People with mortgages or rent to pay. People with tables that need food. People with cars that need fuel, repairs, and insurance. Please do not misread this: I am not suggesting that organizations should never release or lay off someone; I am not suggesting that at all. What I am suggesting is that organizations of any type would be well served if they remembered, every day, that it is all about people. If we can agree that organizations are people, then what is the greatest example of communicating respect, love, and care for people? Empathy, rooted in fully listening and fully understanding.

Two of the greatest threats to empathy in organizations may not be what immediately comes to mind. First, assumptions. Assumptions are one of the cancers of organizational cultural health. Assumptions, when acted upon, often result in bewilderment, hurt, and broken relationships. There is a classic saying about making assumptions that I don't need to repeat here; however, the point is as true today as when those words were first spoken: making assumptions often leads to incorrect conclusions, improper decisions, and hurtful endings.

The second threat is gossip. Gossip is another cancer of organizational cultural health. Gossip undermines, it plants lies and deceit in the minds of the people participating, and it grows molehills into mountains. How do you deal with assumptions and gossip before they spread to the point of turning the culture toxic? With assumptions, you refuse to act on them. You discipline yourself to ask questions, to go directly to the person and have a conversation, and you don't make decisions until you are sure it is factually based on a complete perspective, not an incomplete one. With gossip, when you hear it or hear of it, go to the person and offer three alternatives: (1) mandate that the person gossiping goes to the person being talked about; (2) offer to go with the person gossiping to meet with the person being talked about; or (3) communicate that you will be going to the person being talked about immediately following that conversation unless they choose option one or two first. If assumptions and gossip are not addressed and rooted out, then they will be permitted. Whatever is not addressed will be deemed acceptable, and this will lead to a widespread outbreak of undesirable behaviors and attitudes.

What about you? How have you handled assumptions and gossip in your organization? How about in your personal life? What is your strategy for addressing assumptions and gossip in your organization? How about your personal life?

Now that we have unpacked empathy—what it is, what it isn't, and threats to empathy in organizations—it is time to continue our journey. In the next chapter, our journey takes us to the second part of the un-formula formula: empowerment.

CHAPTER 5

EMPOWERMENT

Have you have ever been frustrated, feeling like you were not allowed to do what you were hired to do? Or have you ever had to ask for permission for something that you believed you had the authority to decide? Or maybe you felt frustration because you used to be able to do something with one person's approval, but it now requires several or even a committee of people to sign off? If you have ever had any of these thoughts or feelings, more likely than not, you were thinking about "empowerment." But when was the last time you thought about empowerment? How about being empowered? Or empowering someone else? While the word "empowerment" is not something you most likely think about on a daily or even semiregular basis, chances are the derivatives of empowerment are more pervasive in your thinking and vocabulary than you may realize. Empowerment is a word that carries both positive and negative connotations. As stated earlier, Merriam-Webster defines empowerment as *the granting of the power, right, or authority to perform various acts or duties* or *the power, right, or authority to do something*. Trying to delineate the differences of connotations of empowerment is beyond the scope of this book. I will limit the focus of empowerment here to the dictionary definition alone.

Take a moment and reread the definition of empowerment, one phrase at a time.

- *The granting of the power, right, or authority.* As a leader, when was the last time you truly granted power to those who report to you—power to do the job that they were hired, trained, equipped, and capable of doing? One of the mistakes leaders make—especially inexperienced, immature, or insecure leaders—is hiring capable leaders and then not "granting the power, right, or authority" to do what they were hired to do.

  What about you? Can you think of any current examples of people who work directly for you who may not feel like they have the power, right, or authority to do their job? What about others in your organization, regardless of whom they report to? What do you need to do to grant the power, right, or authority to these people so they feel the freedom and the ability to perform their job duties fully?

- *The power, right, or authority to do something.* Much like the first part of the definition, the primary difference is the one granting the authority (first part of the definition) versus the one who believes they have the authority to act (second part of the definition).

  What about you? Is there anything in your current role where you have the authority to act or decide but you are not exercising that authority? Why

aren't you? What can you do about this to start acting with the authority you have been granted?

The key to empowerment comes down to one word: *action*. Giving empowerment and being empowered means that the authority to act and decide has been granted. Now, go act! Two of the biggest mistakes leaders make is (1) being granted empowerment to act but then not acting, or (2) not being granted empowerment to act but acting anyway. Both scenarios lead to suboptimal results and often contribute to an unhealthy, potentially toxic culture. Let's return to Paul's story as he unpacks the second part of his conversation with Emma, this time focusing on empowerment.

The day after Paul's morning conversation with Emma, he awoke early in the morning filled with excitement at the thought of diving back into his conversation from a day earlier. As Paul pulled into the parking lot, he was greeted by his friend and boss. "Morning, Paul," Jude waved and exclaimed to Paul.

"Morning, Jude. How are you doing this fine morning?" asked Paul. It was a cool, crisp morning in early November. Fall was in the air. This would be Paul and Patty's first fall in the Nashville area. They were looking forward to a milder winter than the brutal winters that can be experienced in northern Indiana.

"How has the team been doing since our lunch, Paul?" Jude inquired.

"I've had some great team meetings and one-on-ones, Jude. I think the team is really bonding, and I'm excited to be able share the thinking we're putting together as we memorialize the culture that sets Global Solutions apart," Paul replied.

"Can you give me the forty-thousand-foot view?" Jude asked.

Over the next few minutes, Paul gave Jude a high-level overview of his conversation with Emma and the subsequent download he was doing as he typed up his notes. "I'm really excited about this, Paul!" Jude exclaimed excitedly. "This is exactly what I was hoping you would do when you came here. Keep up the great work! I look forward to seeing what you and the team come up with," Jude continued as he walked toward his office. Paul walked into his own office and settled in as he began to type. He had reserved the entire morning to work on getting these notes typed up. He wanted to bring this to the team by the following Monday at their weekly team meeting. He was so excited that he became frustrated that his fingers wouldn't type as fast as he read the notes.

Paul started typing where he left off the morning prior. Empowerment was the second word he wrote down as part of the three "Es" associated with building engaged and excited teams.

Paul had asked Emma if the process of onboarding new employees was the same as what he had experienced. Emma shared with him that each new employee went through a thorough and rigorous onboarding process. The onboarding was primarily focused on culture training and inculcation. After the organizational culture training portion concluded, the next phase was to invest time in training, equipping, teaching, and coaching the employee in his or her specific job role. Once the employee could perform the job they had been hired to do, they would be released to do it. Paul stood up from his desk and walked over to his whiteboard. He wrote the following words:

- Recruit
- Hire
- Onboard

- Equip:
    - Teaching
    - Training
    - Practicing
    - Coaching
- Empower
- Accountable (for Results)
- Continual Learning:
    - Improvement
    - Learning and Growth
    - Advancement

Paul began pacing in his office again. He thought to himself, *What is the best way to empower our team? Is this (the notes on my whiteboard) the process of empowering? What is missing in this process?* Paul continued to pace and to think. There was a knock on his door that startled him out of his processing. "What are you working on?" Jude asked.

"Hey, chief! I'm still unpacking and processing what I shared with you at a high level this morning," Paul answered.

"Great! I was hoping you would be," Jude replied. "Can you walk me through what you have on your whiteboard and what you're thinking about as you wear out your carpet pacing around like you are?" Jude joked.

"How long were you standing there?" Paul sheepishly asked.

"Long enough, my friend!" Jude laughed.

Paul started the conversation, "Imagine this…Global Solutions, Inc.: Building a culture of flourishing individuals, which builds a flourishing organization." Paul and Jude spent the next ninety minutes together discussing what it meant to build a flourishing culture where their team members flourished. They discussed many concepts and ideas, but they finally narrowed the scope down to the following: empathy—caring genuinely; empowerment—trusting fully; excellence—granting authority and responsibility to do the jobs they were hired to do, make decisions, and complete their jobs with excellence.

As Jude stood up to leave, he walked over to Paul, put his arm around his shoulders, pulled him close, and said, "Paul, I am so thrilled you're here! What you're working on is not only amazing for our organization, but it is and will be even more life-changing for our team members. I'm so excited, my friend!"

Paul, at a little over six feet tall and built like a football linebacker, had tears coming to his eyes. "Jude," he finally choked out, "I have never—and I do mean *never*—been told that by any boss in any place I've worked." At this point, Paul had tears fully streaming down his face, "I've never felt this wanted, appreciated, cared for, and empowered to do the job I was hired to do. I was hesitant—really hesitant—to come work for one of my best friends. I must tell you, so far it has been one of the best decisions of my life. Thank you!" Paul finished, his voice cracking and giving out as he choked back his emotions.

"Paul, the day you accepted this role was one of the happiest days of my life," Jude responded with tears also streaming down his face. "Being able to work with one of my best friends whom I've loved and admired for years has been one of the greatest experiences of my life. Regardless of if we work together for a few months, a few years, or for the rest of our careers, you will always be one of my best friends," Jude finished, his voice also choked off by his emotions. The two men embraced, and Jude walked back to his office. Paul sat down for a minute to collect his thoughts. Then, he stood back up and resumed his pacing.

Over the next couple of hours, Paul worked through the process it would take to train the team—especially the team leaders, senior leaders, and executive leaders—in what it means to fully empower team members to do their jobs. When he was done, the process looked like this.

What does empowerment mean at Global Solutions?

- Recruiting and Hiring.
    - Global Solutions must have the most thorough and robust recruiting and hiring process possible. From the first contact with candidates, they must know three things: (1) we want to know them; (2) they are cared for, regardless of if they ever come to work here or not; and (3) they will be part of a team that cares about their learning, growth, and success—being able to do the job they are being hired to do with excellence.
- Onboarding.
    - Once a team member is hired, the onboarding process must be the most thorough and robust process we have as an organization. Onboarding is so critical because that is the individual's first impression and exposure to this organization. We only have one opportunity to make a first impression and to onboard team members to ensure they are properly inculcated into the Global Solutions culture.
    - Starting day one, team members must know, "We were expecting you and we are thrilled you are here

with us!" There will be a welcome package waiting for them on their desk or workspace. We will send a gift to their significant other, if they have one.

- Each team member will spend the first couple of days learning the basics of the organization and getting oriented to things like the copy room, their computers, login information, email setup, break room areas, and the like.
- Each team member will be assigned a "culture coach" who will walk with them during their onboarding and be available for questions, information, debriefing, and relationship building. The culture coach will meet with the new recruit weekly during the onboarding process. For the first six months, we will rotate coaches every month, so each team member gets to know people from different areas.
- As part of the onboarding process, each team member will have a rotation through every department within the company. We want our team members to understand the why and the what of what we do. We want them to see how their individual job contributes to their team success and the success of this company.
- After each ninety days, we will do a check-in evaluation to make sure that each team member is learning, growing, and connecting relationally, and making sure that they are understanding the company, their role, and how they contribute to the long-term success of this company. It is critically important to make sure that our team members are connecting with other

team members and making a friend (or friends) as quickly as possible.

- Equipping.
    - Teaching. Each team member will be part of a continual growth and learning process. We will divide the company into cohorts of five or six with an assigned leader for each group. We will come together every other month for half a day with half the cohorts and have the other half the other month. We will have times of teaching, primarily focused on culture learning, with breakout sessions in cohorts for discussion and application. In between meetings, each cohort will work through a book that is foundational to the culture of Global Solutions.
    - Training. We must have the most thorough training processes and procedures possible. Training for each team member's role is critical, but it is just as critical to provide training for team members who desire to advance in their careers. We also must have a process in place for providing training for skills—both hard and soft—so our team members can improve.
    - Practicing. Training is only as good as the results it generates. If our training does not lead to our team members being able to do their jobs with excellence, we have a training problem, not a team member problem (assuming we have done our hiring effectively). Before a team member is fully released into their role, they will spend time practicing their roles with an assigned supervisor who knows the role

inside and out. The supervisor will observe the team member as they practice, providing coaching and help as needed along the way.

- Coaching. Instilling a culture of coaching is a must if we are serious about sustainable organizational health and having engaged and excited team members. Instilling the mindset of "everyone is a coach; everyone is coached" is a must, with one caveat. "Coaching" is often a euphemism for "confront," "chastise," or "correct." Coaching at Global Solutions absolutely must be focused on helping our team members become the best versions of themselves they can be. When, not if, a conversation of a confronting, chastising, or correcting nature is necessary, we will truthfully call it what it is. As part of our training, we will train in the methodology of *Crucial Conversations*[5] and *Crucial Confrontations*[6] for those times when more direct conversations are warranted. The rest of the time, coaching conversations will be focused on "iron sharpening iron" conversations.

- Empowering.
  - What does it mean to empower the team members at Global Solutions? It means this: when each team member is released to do their job, they will have the training, tools, skills, knowledge, and ability to do

---

[5] Joseph Grenny et al., *Crucial Conversations: Tools for Talking When Stakes Are High* (New York: McGraw-Hill, 2002).

[6] Jospeh Grenny et al., *Crucial Confrontations: Tools for Resolving Broken Promises, Violated Expectations, and Bad Behavior* (New York: McGraw-Hill, 2004).

the job they were hired to do. Furthermore, they will have the authority and responsibility to do their job with excellence. Regardless of role, position, or title, every team member at Global Solutions will be given the authority and the responsibility to do their job with excellence. If a team member does not feel like they have what they need to be successful in their role, the cause of that will come down to one of two reasons: (1) we failed our team member in preparing them or empowering them fully for their roles, or (2) we failed in our hiring process and have a team member in the wrong seat on the proverbial bus. Either way, we must have an open and honest culture that encourages the kinds of conversations where this information is discussed openly and quickly.

- Accountability.
  - Empowerment is not complete without accountability. Empowerment, by definition, means granting authority and conveying responsibility. With authority and responsibility also comes accountability; otherwise, the process breaks down. Whenever a team member is empowered, they must also have accountability to produce results. If a team member is not achieving results, then it is critical to focus on the right issues; this means not focusing on the missed results. When results are missed, the temptation is to emphasize the missed results and start mandating more work, additional hours, or harder effort. The proper priority is to examine the inputs and activities first. If there are insufficient resources or

improper inputs, it will lead to insufficient activities. If there are insufficient or improper activities, there will be insufficient results. Too much time, energy, and effort are spent focusing on the results, which leads to compounded frustration when future results do not improve, even with greater effort. Discipline is required to stop, take three giant steps back, and examine the problem from all angles—starting with inputs and activities. This must be paramount in our training and development throughout the organization.

- Continual Learning. Continual learning must be foundational to the sustainability and scalability of Global Solutions. We must instill this mindset from top to bottom. It is only with the commitment to continually learn that will we remain relevant and competitive in an ever-changing world. The components of continual learning must be taught and trained throughout this organization.
    - Improvement. Each day presents an opportunity to improve; they may be microimprovements, but they are improvements, nonetheless. The reality is that our competitors focus on how to do their business better than we do ours. So, we must have the same focus on improving that other companies do, or we will fall behind. In fact, we must have an even greater commitment to improvement than our competition.
    - Learning and Growth. Continual learning means learning *and* growing. In addition to providing internal opportunities for our team members to learn and grow, we must also provide external opportunities.

We will have a tuition reimbursement program, seminar and workshop opportunities, and other training occasions available to make sure that our team members stay relevant, sharp, and on the leading edge in their respective fields.

- Advancement. While not everyone has the desire to advance, take higher-level jobs, or move up in their career, many do. It is crucial that we provide opportunities and career paths for our team members who desire to advance in their roles and careers. These conversations will start as part of the onboarding process. Each team member will have an annual individual development plan (IDP) that lays out the personal and professional growth goals for the upcoming year. The plan will not be coming up with sixteen professional goals and twenty-three personal goals; the plan will be one or two of each per year, and that is it. If there are more than two or three goals in any given year, the reality is that none will be accomplished.

Paul stopped typing. He looked back over what he had typed up, which was a blend of what he and Emma had discussed and his own thinking. Paul couldn't wait to move on to "excellence," but for today, he had to move on to other meetings and tasks at hand. Paul saved his work, turned off his computer, and exhaled loudly. It had been one of the best mornings of his professional life.

Empowerment. While many organizations have struggled over time to see the relevance of empathy in organizational culture, the concept and practice of empowerment has been around for decades. The issue has less to do with understanding empowerment and is more about putting it into practice.

> **What about you? Do you struggle with empowering those who work for you—in the way that has been defined here? What aspects of empowering others do you struggle with? Have you experienced a time in your career when you did not feel empowered? What did that feel like? What did you do about it?**

As a reminder, keep notes of your answers to these questions along the journey. The answers will be helpful in Part III where we integrate our journey into practical applications and exercises.

Two of the greatest threats to creating a culture of empowerment are control and trust. A classic example of what not to do when organizations hire leaders—especially senior and executive leaders—is hiring them, and then not empowering them with the authority and responsibility to successfully do the job. Often, the reasons for not fully releasing team members to do their jobs are rooted in the desire to retain control and in a lack of trust.

When a leader struggles to empower and the root cause is the desire to retain control, that leader has two options. First, that leader's direct reports move to another supervisor, and the leader who struggles with empowerment is relegated to an individual contributor. Leaders who must retain and keep control are not team players. Control has an indirect correlation with growth—both organizational and team members' growth. The more an organization grows, the more the leaders in that organization must share authority and responsibility, which are the core of empowerment. Without the sharing of authority and responsibility, leaders who retain control for decision-making, signoffs, approvals, and reviews create bottlenecks. As a result of these bottlenecks, organizational growth is limited to the capacity of that leader's (or those leaders', if more than one) capacity. The second option for a leader who must retain control is removing the leader—either voluntarily or involuntarily. If the leader is not removed, the leaders and direct reports under that control-oriented leader will grow increasingly frustrated, helpless, and angry, increasing the likelihood of departure severalfold from that organization. Over time, a control-oriented leader will not be able to retain leaders who were hired into leadership roles, because those new leaders will feel powerless to lead. There is a third viable option for consideration, but it is much less common and happens infrequently. The option is that the leader agrees to intensives in counseling and coaching to deal with the root causes associated with that leader's control issues.

When a leader struggles to empower and the root cause is a lack of trust, that leader also has two options. First, the leader must evaluate the root cause issues related to mistrust. If a leader struggles to trust anyone, more than likely the root cause is within that leader; however, if the leader easily trusts, but then struggles to trust a certain individual, the leader would be well served to spend time with the person he or she struggles with to dive into the possible issues. Some people have an intuitive gut feeling about certain situations and people. Sometimes those gut feelings are warranted, sometimes not. If trust issues remain after spending time getting to know the person, the individual may need to be moved to another team or released from the organization. While that may seem unfair or like it's an extreme response, if a supervisor cannot trust a team member, it is not fair to the person who is not trusted, the other team members, or the supervisor to keep someone in a leadership role when that leadership will be questioned by the supervisor. It is better for all if that person is removed from that situation. Second, if a leader struggles with trusting other people in general, but really struggles trusting their direct reports, that leader must be addressed. Options to address issues with trust could be counseling, coaching, trust-related exercises, and other therapies. If a leader who struggles with trust is not addressed, mistrust grows and spreads like a cancer within teams and then to the organization overall.

> **What about you? Do you struggle with a need for control? What have you done to address this in your life? Do you struggle with trust? What have you done to address this?**

Leaders who struggle with the need for control and who struggle to trust others will have limited effectiveness in their leadership impact. Leaders with the mindset of learning and growing who are willing to grow beyond their need for control or trust issues not only see their effectiveness grow as a leader but also see their impact grow with their teams and the organization overall.

In this chapter, Paul and Jude introduced a new concept of what it means to build a culture of engaged and excited teams: building flourishing individuals who build flourishing organizations. In the next chapter, our journey moves to the third and final component of the un-formula formula for building engaged and excited teams: excellence.

CHAPTER 6

EXCELLENCE

Have you ever been part of a team—whether football, soccer, basketball, softball, baseball, swimming, academics, Bible quizzing, debate, project, department, leadership, executive, or any other team you can think of? Did your team win? Did it have a habit of winning? Or did your team struggle to win? Being part of team competition in high school or college often generates memories that last for a lifetime. Memories of the last-second shot as the ball fell through the hoop as time expired on the clock, giving your team the one-point win, elicits smiles, hollers, and excited story-telling many years past its occurrence. Memories of the "Hail Mary" pass into the end zone with the opposing team down by five as their tallest player leapt above all the others as time expired; when the huddle was unraveled and all the players removed, there lay the ball, neatly nestled in the arms of the opposing player. Touchdown! Heartbreak! The story, even years later, elicits tears with the memory of being mere seconds away from the state championship game.

Being part of sports or academic teams in school gives way to being part of project, department, or leadership teams in organizations. Sports teams experience the thrill of victory and the agony of defeat; so do organizational teams. The circumstances are obviously different, the opponent is different, and the objectives are different; however, the fundamental goals are the same—be excellent, do right, and win. But two trends tend to happen over time in teams: less focus and a decreased commitment to excellence. The reasons that focus and commitment to excellence tend to decline over time are severalfold; however, one of the core reasons is leadership reducing emphasis of the vision, mission, and purpose of the existence of the team or the organization. The natural momentum of organizations is away from their original vision, mission, and purpose. Time has a way of softening commitment, causing distraction, and reducing discipline. Without a constant and consistent reminder of the original intent and purpose, teams and organizations naturally lose focus and drift away from their stated purpose. In their book *Mission Drift*, Greer and Horst unpack this phenomenon of teams and organizations "drifting" away from the original intent, purpose, and focus of the founding leaders.[7] As teams and organizations drift from their purpose, something else occurs at the same time: loss of motivation, excitement, and commitment to excellence. What was once not tolerated is suddenly tolerated—even encouraged. What was once considered unacceptable is suddenly acceptable. What was once disciplined is now permitted. If not corrected, the natural slide away from vision, mission, and purpose is toward increasing tolerance for errors, mistakes, attitudes, and behaviors that were not previously tolerated. As organizational culture migrates, team members become less excited, less committed, and less excellent.

---

[7] Peter Greer and Chris Horst, *Mission Drift: The Unspoken Crisis Facing Leaders, Charities, and Churches* (Bloomington, MN: Bethany House Publishers, 2015).

The result is that organizational results become increasingly less excellent; mediocrity, and the acceptance of it, becomes the new cultural norm.

While the natural course of organizational culture and performance may be away from the original vision, mission, and purpose of the organization, it does not have to be this way. Just because the natural course of things is toward chaos and away from order does not mean that it must be this way. To stay true to the original intent and vision, mission, and purpose, organizational leadership must be intentional, consistent, and repetitive. Excellence in organizations is the same; it takes intentionality, consistency, and repetition to keep individuals motivated to do their very best day in and day out. Now, let's get back to Paul.

Patty was waiting for Paul at the door when he walked in the house. Paul had just completed his best workday ever, as he had described it to Patty when they talked on the phone on his drive home. Patty was waiting with excited anticipation to hear all about his day. As Paul slid his backpack off his shoulder and removed his coat, Patty couldn't wait any longer. "So, tell me! What happened today that made this your 'best workday ever'?" Patty asked. "I want to hear all about it." For years, Patty had seen the light in Paul's eyes go from bright, to faded, to all but dimmed; she had seen the life in her husband gradually get sucked from him as day after day he faithfully put in his time working in an unhealthy, toxic organizational culture. Patty had seen her husband's confidence in both himself and in his abilities wane to all but nothing. She had not seen her husband excited to go to work in the morning in years; she had never seen him return home in the evening after work with that excitement having grown even stronger than when he left in the morning.

After their brief conversation during Paul's drive home, Patty had laid down her phone, walked to her favorite chair by the fireplace in the living room, and let her tears flow freely down her cheeks. She had softly whispered, "Thank you, Jesus, for providing this for Paul—for us. After all the years of struggling, stress, anxiety, and bewilderment, Paul is a different man; he is a new man. I am so grateful, Lord. In Jesus's name, Amen." Patty had kept her eyes closed for several moments after she finished praying. She had cried softly—tears of joy. She had smiled slightly, genuinely happy, and held her hands open wide—truly grateful.

After Paul took off his shoes and had a moment to change his clothes, he started relaying the events of the day to Patty. They laughed, they cried, they embraced as Paul recounted everything that had happened. "Patty, it seems like this isn't even reality—like any moment, it seems as though everything is going to change, and it will be like it used to be," Paul said as he concluded his story from the day.

"I understand what you're feeling, Paul. I have the same feelings too; however, we must trust Jesus that this is different—truly different!" Patty responded. "We have waited, we have prayed, we have sought counsel, and we have been faithful, Paul. I don't believe that if we do 'A+B+C' that God will do 'D+E+F.' I am just saying that we did not make the decision to uproot our kids and move five hundred miles away from the only home we ever knew on a whim. We believe fully that this is where we are supposed to be, where we have been called to be." Patty's voice faded as she choked back another round of happy tears.

Paul had big tears filling his eyes as well, and as he closed them and let the tears roll down his cheeks, he pulled Patty in close and whispered, "We are home, my love. We are home. I love you! Thank you for being on this journey with me." They stood in silence for a few moments until Paul's stomach rumbled loudly.

"Wow! You hungry, dear?" Patty asked.

"You know, I completely forgot to eat lunch today! I was so excited and focused that I completely forgot to eat," Paul laughed. Patty and Paul went to the kitchen to prepare some food to eat. They spent the rest of the evening chatting and watching one of their favorite shows before turning in early for bed.

The next day, Paul was up early once again and pulled into the office parking lot by 6:45 a.m. He was one of the only ones in the office at that time of the day, which was something he was becoming quite fond of. As he laid his backpack down and pulled off his coat, he noticed the bookshelf in his office. Sitting in a prominent place on the shelf was the Bible he had owned for over thirty years: a leather-bound version of the New American Standard Bible. It had been a couple of weeks since Paul had spent time alone with God, reading the Bible. He grabbed the Bible, opened it to Matthew 5, and read through Jesus's Sermon on the Mount. Paul spent fifteen minutes reading, followed by another fifteen minutes in prayer to start his day. Praying through the Lord's Prayer from Matthew 6 was one of Paul's fondest ways to pray in his time with God. He closed his prayer by expressing his gratitude for all that had transpired from his last job through that day, and he asked God for wisdom and insight for his day. After his time with God, Paul powered on his computer, erased his whiteboard, and prepared himself for diving into the final component of building engaged and excited teams—flourishing individuals building a flourishing organization.

Excellence, Paul wrote on his whiteboard. "What is excellence, *really*?" Paul muttered to himself. He then wrote the following phrases about excellence on his whiteboard:

- Excellence = results
- Excellence = performance

- Excellence = mindset
- Excellence = commitment
- Excellence = discipline
- Excellence = consistency
- Excellence = culture
- Excellence = way of life

Paul sat at the small, round table in his office, stared at his whiteboard for a while, and pondered what these phrases meant and how they were related. After a while of thinking and doodling in his notebook, he stood up and walked back to the whiteboard where he wrote:

> *Excellence is a mindset that builds a culture where discipline and commitment lead to consistent performance and results.*

Paul sat back down and read the sentence to himself and then aloud probably twenty times. "But what builds the mindset of excellence?" Paul asked himself aloud. He went back to the whiteboard and wrote:

> *The mindset of excellence: leaders communicating and living the vision, mission, and purpose of the organization with an unwavering commitment to building a culture of flourishing individuals building flourishing organizations.*

Paul thought about his short tenure at Global Solutions. He recalled the interviews, the conversations, and the relationships he had established in such a short time. He recalled the conversations he'd had with Jude both before coming and since coming.

As he thought fondly about his time in his new role, something became clear to him. Jude, the leaders, and now most of the team members in this organization care about each other's flourishing—genuinely and authentically. When people are cared for and they, in turn, care for others, there is a contagious effect that spreads through the entire organization. The team members here are known, wanted, and cared for; they are excited to come to work because of the blessings that have been given to them. Sure, pay and benefits are good, but the culture and the mindset of the team here has little or nothing to do with pay and benefits; it has to do with flourishing. The team is flourishing; the organization is flourishing. The team is excellent; the organization is excellent. That is the "secret sauce" of this place!

Paul's mind was racing now as he continued to ponder and reflect. Excellence is more than a mindset, however; excellence also means having excellent practices that are repeatable, sustainable, and scalable as the organization grows. Global Solutions has taken the time to meticulously detail each role, each job, and each process, not to make everything as rote and routine as possible but to make best practices and expectations fully known. This organization cares enough to provide the opportunity for each team member to do their best and to reach their potential in whatever they do. Paul thought through the role descriptions, process manuals, and standard operating procedures for each area of the organization. They were simple to understand, contained best practices, and were up-to-date and relevant. When team members discovered a new or better way of doing something, they were not chastised or discouraged for doing it differently; they were encouraged to share their discoveries so the processes could be updated with a better way of doing things. This created a sense of ownership for every team member and for every role in the organization. Each team member met with their supervisor every week or every other week, depending upon the role, for a one-hour one-on-one. For the first half hour, the time was the team member's time to discuss whatever they wanted. The second half hour was the supervisor's time to discuss whatever they wanted. Often, these one-on-ones would be a blend of job-related topics, personal topics, growth, learning, and coaching. When there was new learning or there were improvements in existing practices to be shared, those discussions often occurred in one-on-one conversations or anytime that a team member wanted to share their learning.

Paul then thought about how an organization builds a culture of excellence that is sustainable over time. Paul's mind went to accountability. All team members are held and willing to be held accountable for both their responsibilities and their results. Feedback is provided in real time along with scheduled times throughout the year. The difference here with quarterly or annual reviews is that there are no surprises; the conversations—especially those related to performance improvement—had already taken place. As a result, scheduled reviews were just that: reviews—reviews of current progress, learning, growth, and results. Annually, each team member puts together their IDP—individual development plan. Unlike any place Paul had ever been, those IDPs are taken seriously. Each team member has a budget allocated to them for learning and growth, and each team member sets only one or two professional and personal development goals. Every place Paul had ever been before had required more like five to ten goals, and always professional, not personal. This place cares about these team members' personal goals as well as professional, Paul realized. *No wonder these team members are loyal, hard-working, focused, and committed to excellence in everything*, he thought.

After Paul finished thinking, he started typing. Two hours later, he was satisfied that he had properly recalled and memorialized his thoughts regarding excellence. After he finished typing and saved his work, Paul leaned back in his chair. He sighed a sigh of both relief and anticipation. Relief at the feeling of satisfaction that he had properly captured his conversation with Emma and effectively expanded that conversation with his evaluation and observation of Global Solutions since he started. Anticipation about the feeling of now having to figure out the next phase: *what does it mean to build flourishing individuals who build flourishing organizations?* That was the next mountain to climb in figuring out and documenting the process for creating a healthy, engaged culture where people are excited to come to work because they are shown empathy, they are empowered, and they produce excellence. *Flourishing individuals build flourishing organizations,* Paul wrote on his whiteboard as he walked out of his office.

Excellence. Being part of something excellent—whether that's business, sports, community, church, music, or something else—is fun. When something is less than excellent, mediocre even, and it is tolerated—or worse, encouraged—it often produces frustration, angst, and possibly anger. What Paul was experiencing at Global Solutions was an organization that not only produced excellent results but also an organizational culture that created the mindset and commitment for excellence. It is one thing to produce excellence once, or once-in-a-while; however, to produce excellence in a consistent and sustainable fashion day in and day out is another feat entirely. Paul had experienced excellence before, but not like what he saw at Global Solutions. As he processed and documented his thinking, it provided a great road map for us in our journey to build upon as we seek to build organizations that are excellent, produce excellent results, and do this day in and day out.

> **What about you? Have you experienced excellence being part of a team? What was that experience like for you? Have you experienced mediocrity or something less than excellence in being part of a team? What was that experience like?**

In Part II, we will unpack the Flourishing Life Model for individuals in the context of organizations and building flourishing organizations. Before we move on to the second part of our journey, let's step back for a moment and look at our map to see where we have been and where we are going. We started our journey by examining the problem of unengaged teams. We then discussed the "un-formula" formula for building engaged and excited teams. The formula included empathy, empowerment, and excellence. Along the journey of discovering the process of building engaged and excited teams, we discovered another way of defining engaged and excited teams: *flourishing organizations.* The process of building flourishing organizations is rooted in building flourishing individuals, where we are currently on the map of our journey.

The next leg of our journey takes us into Part II, the Flourishing Life Model, applied to building flourishing organizations. Then, our final stop will take us to Part III, where we will learn practical and simple-to-understand practices and exercises for building flourishing organizations of engaged and excited teams. Are you ready to move on to Part II? Let's go!

PART II

CHAPTER 7

THE FLOURISHING LIFE MODEL

When was the last time you looked forward to going to work because you enjoyed it there? When did you roll out of bed on a Monday morning and think to yourself, *I am so stoked for another work week*? While it is not realistic to expect that every Monday, every week, or every day you will be excited to go to work, it *is* realistic to expect that, for the most part, going to work will be a pleasant experience—and not something to be dreaded. When you are flourishing, it means you are operating where your passion, skills, gifts, contribution to others, and calling intersect in your life. When this intersection occurs, you operate at a level where you are living with meaning, and you understand your purpose in life. When organizations are intentional about taking the time and investing the resources in their team members to help them discover their path to flourishing, in turn they build an organization that flourishes. The graphic below, first introduced in *unSatisfied: When Less Is More,* depicts the "intersection" mentioned above.

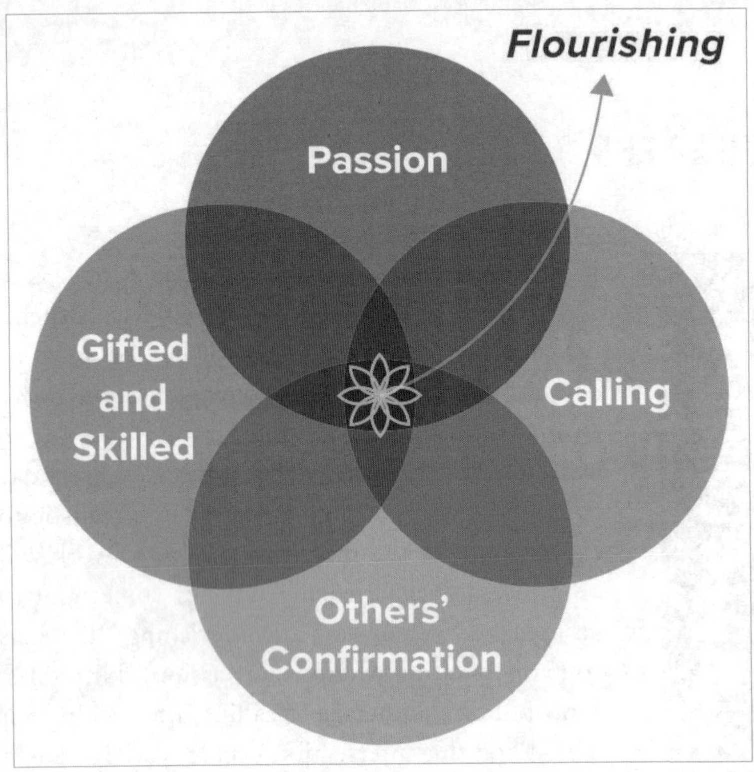

In the book *unSatisfied: When Less Is More,* I introduced the Flourishing Life Model to the world. I developed this model after decades of working with leaders and leadership teams all over the world, and leading others. I discovered that no matter the country or the culture, there was a common thread woven through the way many led their organizations, built their businesses, and lived their lives. I spent years trying to figure out this "thread" that I had observed time and time again. Over time, the thread evolved into a triangle with four levels, but it felt incomplete. I wrestled for years with why it felt incomplete and could not find a satisfactory answer. So, I waited. Two years before *unSatisfied* was published, the fifth and top layer of the Flourishing Life Model became known and real to me. Finally, I started writing.

For the context of this book, The Flourishing Life Model has been adapted specifically to organizations and organizational life. I would encourage you to read *unSatisfied: When Less Is More* to more fully understand the original definitions of the levels of the model, as well as the barriers and accelerators to each. While the terminology of the levels is the same in both books, I have adapted the definitions and characteristics to organizational life in this book. This adaptation does not take away from the original characteristics; rather, it adds to and enhances them. As we go through the adapted Flourishing Life Model for creating flourishing organizations, we will continue to follow the story of Paul and Global Solutions.

Paul slept in on Saturday morning, which was very unusual for him. He looked at the clock on his side of the bed. "It's 8:35 a.m! Already?" Paul exclaimed. Paul's normal rhythm on a Saturday was to get out of bed by 6:00, maybe 6:30 at the latest, so he could have a couple of hours for himself before Patty and the kids woke up. He was astonished that he had slept for so long. He lay in bed for a moment and then realized that he heard… nothing. The house was eerily quiet. No one was home. Then, he recalled this was the day that Patty, their three kids, her new friend from church, Alice, and her two kids were helping with clothes and food distribution for those in need around the city. Paul had the house to himself until at least 4:00 p.m.

Paul poured a cup of coffee, put a bagel in the toaster, and sat down on the stool at the bar in the kitchen. He checked his emails and texts. "Nothing. Wow! Quiet day so far," Paul whispered. After Paul finished eating, he went into his study. He sat down at his desk, leaned back in his chair, pulled out his Bible, and started reading. After fifteen minutes of reading and another fifteen minutes praying and journaling, his mind began to drift to the conversations of the past week. He reminisced about the conversations on healthy organizational culture, creating engaged and excited teams, and how flourishing individuals build flourishing organizations. Then, he focused on his task for the day: he needed to figure out how the Flourishing Life Model could be used at Global Solutions to help build flourishing individuals would help build a flourishing organization. Paul began to work through the Flourishing Life Model, adapting it as he went. He started at the bottom of the model, *diminishing*, and worked his way to the top, *flourishing*. He did not change some parts of the definitions because they were still applicable; others, he significantly adapted to make them more relevant to organizational culture. He did not have a whiteboard in his home office, so he pulled out his laptop and started to type.

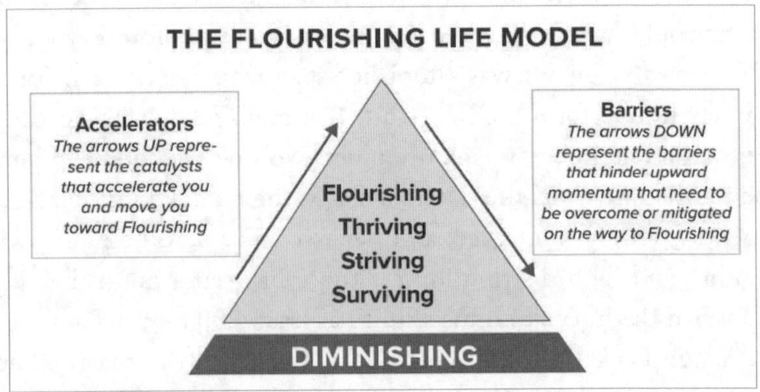

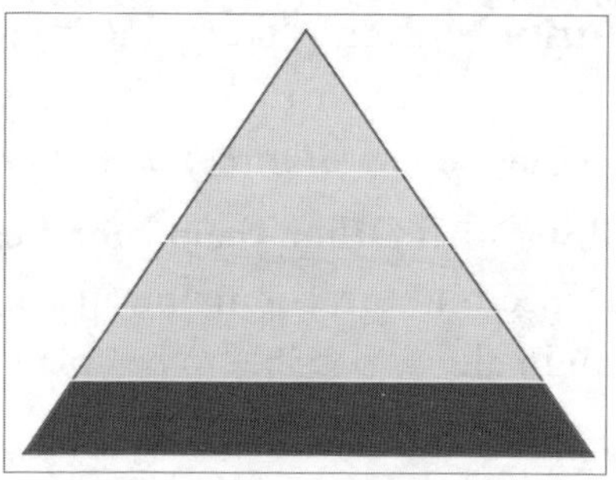

DIMINISHING

Paul started with the bottom level of the model: the *diminishing* level. This is the level where hope is all but lost. Where you have tried and failed and then accepted that failure somehow just became part of who you are. Rather than viewing failure as an event on your journey, being in the *diminishing* level, you view failure as an integral part of your story. For whatever reason, you have lost the ability to separate failure and personhood—who you are as a person—on your journey. The *diminishing* level is where failure, hurt, disappointment, hopelessness, pain, betrayal, and sometimes despair have come to define you. The *diminishing* level is a little below the triangle because those who live at the *diminishing* level often disengage from others or do not see their inherent value or the contribution they bring to others' lives.

What are the characteristics of team members who may be at the diminishing *level?* Paul thought. *I wonder how this relates to engagement, empathy, empowerment, and excellence?* He continued writing.

Characteristics of the DIMINISHING Level

- **Mindset.** Realizes they must work and just want to put in their time; *leave me alone and let me just do my job.*

- **Posture/Attitude.** Don't like going to work, don't like where they work, or don't like who they work with (or some a combination of all three); *I can't stand my job.*
- **Relationships with Other Team Members.** Nonexistent; loner; disrespectful; curt; communicates only when spoken to, or as minimally as possible to be able to do their job.
- **Work/Career.** Feels stuck; little or no motivation to improve or grow.
- **Engagement.** Unengaged; minimal effort; does the least amount possible; not motivated.
- **Empathy.** Does not express empathy, understanding, or caring to team members or supervisors; listens long enough to be able to do their job and then tunes out.
- **Empowerment.** Does not feel empowered and does not empower others; does not ask for nor offer others help with projects or tasks; not collaborative.
- **Excellence.** Does not seek to improve work or quality; does what is told; does not implement feedback or correction, even when necessary.

As Paul finished writing the characteristics and definitions of the *diminishing* level, he thought, *These* characteristics *apply to all levels but with different* definitions. *Those at the* diminishing *level would be those team members with the highest rate of turnover. Ideally, those with this mindset would be filtered out during the recruiting process because their negative attitudes and unwanted behaviors could destructively influence others.*

Paul made a couple of written notes in his notebook regarding the recruiting process to follow up with Emma about on Monday. The Global Solutions hiring team must be sure to ask the right questions during the hiring process to identify and weed out those with a *diminishing* mindset. Paul continued to the *surviving* level.

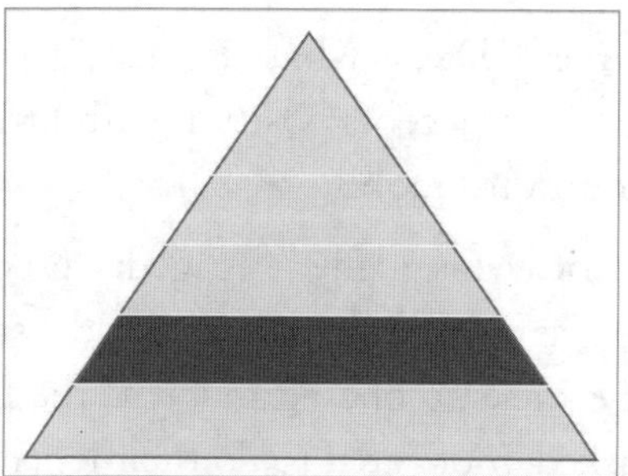

SURVIVING

"What does a team member with a *surviving* mindset look like?" Paul wondered aloud. *Surviving* means doing whatever it takes to ensure that the person is checking the required boxes for their job. Survival is inherent in every living creature or thing on the planet, but what does that look like for people in organizations? Every team member who joins us at Global Solutions would ideally seek to reach the *flourishing* level; however, we must provide the opportunities and path for them to be able to do so. Although *surviving* is a step up from *diminishing*, it is not what we want long term for any of our team members. *What are the characteristics of the* surviving *level?* Paul thought as he wrote.

Characteristics of the SURVIVING Level

- **Mindset.** Seeks and likes routine work; does not actively look for additional work or challenging projects but will accept them if asked; *I am checking the boxes on my to-do list.*

- **Posture/Attitude.** Reliably shows up on time to work every day to do their assigned job; *just another day at the office.*
- **Relationships with Other Team Members.** Functional; task-oriented; cordial but not relational.
- **Work/Career.** Does what is necessary and required; meets deadlines; accepts position with little motivation for growth or upward mobility.
- **Engagement.** Marginally engaged; responds well when asked to do new projects or tasks but doesn't seek them out proactively; sticks to oneself much of the time but will join in when asked; motivated to do their job, but only their job.
- **Empathy.** Expresses little empathy: cares but does not actively seek relationships with other team members; will join in and help if asked but does not volunteer to help, even when it should be obvious.
- **Empowerment.** Feels marginally empowered to do their job; does not feel empowered to do more than their job; rarely, if ever, speaks up, even when improvements or efficiencies are obvious.
- **Excellence.** Does job reliably and effectively; does not actively seek to improve but responds well when given feedback or ways to improve.

Paul finished writing the characteristics of the *surviving* level. *There are* surviving *team members in every organization, and I know that Global Solutions is not the exception*, he thought. *As an organization, it is imperative that we identify these team members by name so we can work with them to help them see the bigger picture for who they are, what they do, and how their contribution matters.* He thought about how important it would be to understand the current motivation of each team member but, more importantly, to understand what their aspirations are—both personally and professionally. *For those who are motivated to grow and advance, we must provide the opportunities for them to learn, grow, and gain the skills and experience they need to do so,* he thought. *For those who are satisfied in their role, that is fine as well; however, we must still provide them opportunities to learn, grow, and fully own their roles.*

Paul made additional notes in his notebook to discuss with Emma about identifying team members at the *surviving* level. He turned back to his computer and moved on to the *striving* level.

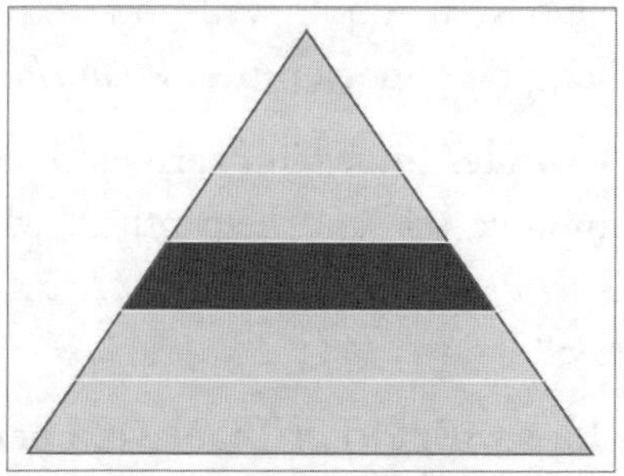

STRIVING

Paul recalled from *unSatisfied:*

> Once you get a glimpse or a taste that there is more to life than *surviving*—and you decide you want to experience more in life—the journey of *striving* has begun. Living a *striving* life is making the decision to change, to grow, to improve, to be different, to be better, and to experience something

different. Making the decision to intentionally make a change and go on the journey is often the most difficult part.[8]

We have to be best-in-class at identifying those team members who have moved from surviving *to* striving, *or are on the verge of doing so*, Paul thought. *We must invest into those team members who desire to grow, learn, and gain new skills and experiences, and give them an opportunity to advance. These team members are motivated, and they see a future for themselves at Global Solutions. It is our responsibility to do whatever it takes to invest in them and prepare them for their journey. What are the characteristics of the* striving *level?* Paul wondered as he typed.

Characteristics of the STRIVING Level

- **Mindset.** Does their job well and actively seeks other, more challenging opportunities; *What else can I do?*
- **Posture/Attitude.** Shows up early and stays late; actively seeks to improve self and help others whenever possible: *How can I get better? What do I need to do to improve? How else can I help?*
- **Relationships with Other Team Members.** Moving from functional to relational; actively seeks new relationships both within the same team and in other teams; may seek to engage with others outside of work as well as inside.
- **Work/Career.** Seeks new challenges and opportunities; sees opportunities to grow and expand in their current role as well as others; committed to the organization for the long term.

---

[8] Matthew Q. Lesser, *unSatisfied: When Less Is More* (Carson City, NV: Lioncrest Publishing, 2022).

- **Engagement.** Experiencing growing engagement; seeks new projects and opportunities, especially if they are outside of their current role and responsibilities; responds enthusiastically when asked to participate in new projects; collaborative team player.
- **Empathy.** Growing level of care for team members; listens effectively; seeks personal and not just professional connections.
- **Empowerment.** Feels fully empowered to perform their own role; feels marginally empowered to seek additional work or new projects; will speak up, on occasion, when better or improved ways to do their own job are discovered; will offer insight to others to help them in their roles.
- **Excellence.** Has a growing commitment to do their job better and with greater excellence; seeks ways to contribute to others' roles to help them improve; growing level of concern for the overall excellence of the organization.

Paul sat back in his chair as he scrolled through and read what he had just written. *We absolutely must identify our* striving *team members*, he thought. Striving *team members are getting it; they see the difference they can make in our organization. They are potential long-term team players. We must do whatever it takes to not just keep them but also invest in them, helping achieve whatever level of success they desire to achieve in our company*. Once again, Paul made sidenotes in his notebook for his Monday discussion with Emma.

Thriving *is next*, Paul thought. "I am looking forward to this one!" he exclaimed aloud.

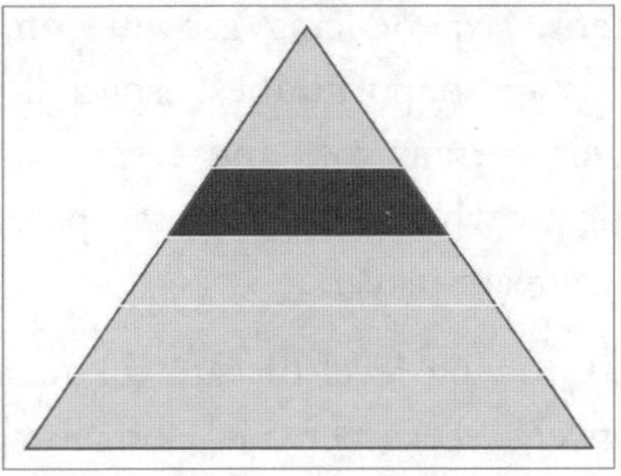

THRIVING

What does thriving *mean at Global Solutions?* Paul wondered. *Wait. The bigger question is: what does* thriving *mean in organizational life, in general?*

Paul recalled from *unSatisfied:*

> *Thriving* is feeling like you are not only effective in a particular role or function, but you are also good at it, and others see and say the same.[9]

"Based on this definition, *thriving,* at Global Solutions, means having team members who not only do their role with excellence, but also, they really enjoy what they do—and their team members will see it!" Paul exclaimed. "Our *thriving* team members are those who love what they do, are proficient at what they do, love their team members, and genuinely care for the organization—both in its current state and its future success as well," Paul wrote. Paul went on to write about the characteristics of the *thriving* level.

[9] Lesser, *unSatisfied.*

Characteristics of the THRIVING Level

- **Mindset.** Does their job with proficiency and excellence; high-level contributor; committed to continual learning and growth; *I have this!*
- **Posture/Attitude.** Confident in both abilities and in getting results; seeks the most challenging problems possible; *I can do it!*
- **Relationships with Other Team Members.** Moves seamlessly from functional to relational in relationships both in and out of work; collaborative but often seeks to be the point person or decision-maker in team projects.
- **Work/Career.** Long-time demonstrated track record of success—especially with challenging and difficult situations and projects; seeks to reach the highest level possible in the organization; seeks to maximize one's career success; committed to the organization for the long term, if opportunities to advance are available.
- **Engagement.** Fully engaged, especially with difficult and challenging projects; demonstrates increasing engagement with increasing level of authority given; seeks advancement opportunities often; collaborative team player—especially when in the point person or decision-maker role.
- **Empathy.** Demonstrates care and concern for fellow team members but does not tolerate nonperforming or underperforming team members well; a good listener, but does not tolerate complaining, whining, or excuse-making.
- **Empowerment.** Feels fully empowered to do own role; feels fully empowered to seek additional work or projects;

holds accountable those teams and team members who are not performing at their full capacity; speaks up when better or improved ways are known or discovered; often shares own successes and ways of doing things, hoping to propel others to higher levels of performance.

- **Excellence.** Fully committed to excellence—especially excellent results; demonstrates lack of patience, at times, with processes—especially when processes seem tedious or slow down progress; laser-focused on the image and brand of the organization as a whole; committed to seeing the organization become all it can be.

As Paul wrapped up the *thriving* characteristics, he decided to scroll back through what he wrote. *The biggest issue with our* thriving *team members is not their performance—because their performance is consistently stellar. The biggest issue is their impact on other team members—especially if team members are struggling or not performing at the same level*, Paul thought. *The commitment to excellence and results from our* thriving *team members is contagious; however, their lack of patience, at times, with some team members can hurt the overall culture of the organization. We want all our team members to reach the* thriving *level; however, the reality is that not all will. How do we emphasize the best of our* thriving *team members and at the same time, help them develop greater empathy for those team members they perceive to not be at their level?* Paul wondered. *Furthermore, how do we keep our* thriving *team members satisfied when we cannot advance them as quickly or as high in the organization as they want to be? It seems like our* thriving *team members, while potentially the highest contributing team members we have, are the highest risk for flight from our organization if we do not give them more, bigger, and better. It also seems like our* thriving *team members can be at risk for burnout.*

Paul wrote some additional notes in his notebook to cover with Emma on Monday. He sat back, stretched his arms, and sighed. "I wonder what lessons I am going to learn from the *flourishing* level that will help me figure out how to not only keep our *thriving* team members, but also keep them fully engaged and begin to adopt the mindset of the *flourishing* level?" Paul asked himself. He leaned forward in his chair and started to dive into the *flourishing* level.

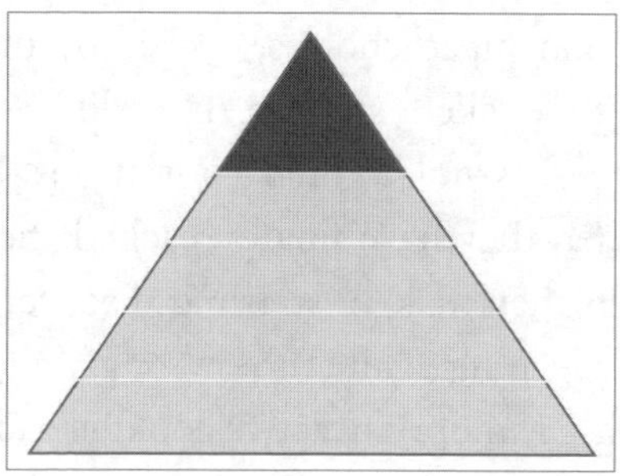

FLOURISHING

What does flourishing *look like in organizational life?* Paul wondered. He read through the "flourishing" section from *unSatisfied* to get some perspective and to remember what it was from a personal perspective. He decided to include a section from the book in his notes as a reference for his team and himself:

> What does it mean to live a *flourishing* life? Eric Liddell, one of the greatest competitive, Olympic runners in history, said, "God made me to run and to run fast. When I run, I feel God's pleasure!"[10] *Flourishing* is *more* than, but it is also *less* than. We live in a culture that says, "Just

[10] *Chariots of Fire*, directed by Hugh Hudson (1981; London: Enigma Productions).

Do It,"[11] "Have It Your Way,"[12] and "Expect More."[13] But what does all this mean? We see the commercials on television. We see the ads in magazines, online, and on billboards. All these messages seem to portray the life we "should" have, "want" to have, or "need" to have. *Really?*

So many people spend their lives climbing the corporate ladder (and that can be in business, nonprofit, church, academia, public service). They climb over and use people and make choices, decisions, and sacrifices every time they take a step up the ladder—sometimes even choosing to violate their convictions, beliefs, and morals. When they have finally reached the top of the ladder, often they make a startling discovery. The ladder is either leaning against the wrong wall, or there is another, higher, more-attractive-looking ladder, or the view from the top was nothing like what they hoped or imagined.

For some, climbing the corporate ladder is exactly what you are called to do. If that is what you are called and equipped to do, you are good at doing it, and you are passionate about doing that, then do it. We need gifted, experienced, and driven leaders who are called and equipped to lead government, academia, business, nonprofits, NGOs, and the arts. And please, do it with all of you and with excellence in all you do. To do anything else will be less than fulfilling for you and will not

[11] Nike slogan, coined in 1988.

[12] Burger King slogan, coined in 1974.

[13] Target slogan ("Expect More. Pay Less."), coined in 1994.

bring you joy. In other words, you will not experience the *flourishing* life if you pursue anything other than what you are equipped, experienced, gifted, and passionate about doing. And if you do pursue that, please make sure that you do it in such a way that you and others are inspired to live a *flourishing* life that causes others to want to do the same.

A life that flourishes is a life that pours out—a life that gives back. A *flourishing* life is a life that lives beyond oneself. A *flourishing* life focuses and thinks beyond this life. A *flourishing* life is a life that is more concerned with legacy, impact, and giving back than with getting, accumulating, and growing in fame and fortune. The *flourishing* life is more concerned with impact and influence over power and prestige. The *flourishing* life is more concerned with giving over getting. The *flourishing* life is more concerned with sacrifice over comfort. The *flourishing* life is more concerned with contributing over consuming. The *flourishing* life is more concerned with experiences over things. The *flourishing* life is more concerned with legacy over temporal. And the *flourishing* life is more concerned with story over CliffsNotes. From a spiritual perspective, a *flourishing* life is more concerned with building God's kingdom over building one's own personal empire.

Summarized, *flourishing* is living a life dedicated to something that is beyond you—it is living a surrendered life to your calling (or to God's calling for you, if you prefer). As I mentioned earlier, *flourishing* is living at the intersection of your passion, what you are gifted and skilled at doing, what has been confirmed and affirmed by others, and your calling.[14]

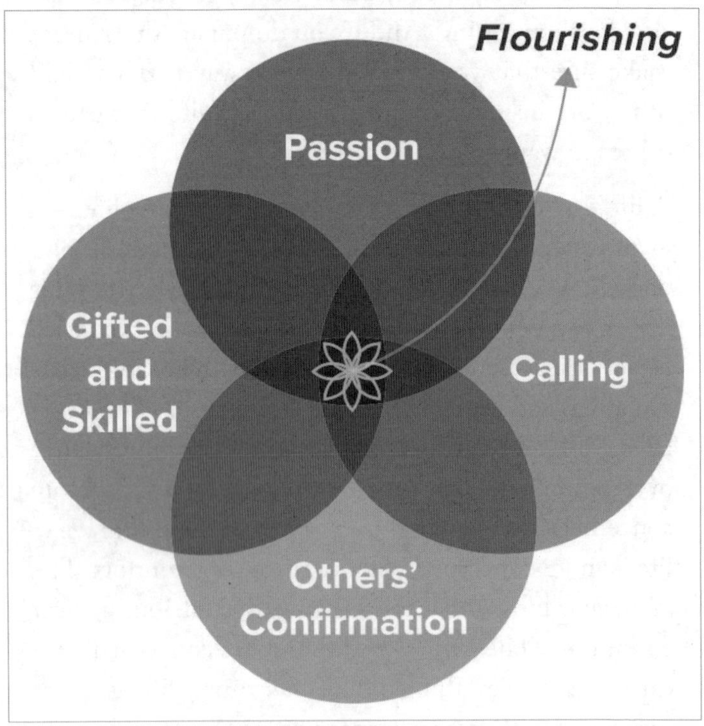

After Paul finished including the excerpts from *unSatisfied*, he thought, *This is what we want at Global Solutions, regardless of our team members' roles. At the end of the day, we want every single team member to be living at the* flourishing *level. We want every team member living at the intersection of their passion, what they are gifted and skilled at doing, what others affirm for them in their doing, and their calling. Not everyone is called to be at the highest*

[14] Lesser, *unSatisfied*.

levels in organizational life—and that is what we must celebrate! Paul thought about how it is way too easy to move aside or dismiss team members who do not seek advancement or desire to move up the corporate ladder. "We need to do everything we can to support those who are passionate and are called to advance, helping them achieve whatever level of success they desire," Paul wrote. "But for those who are content and joyful in what they do, we need to celebrate that just as much!" Paul then continued to write as he laid out the characteristics of the *flourishing* level.

Characteristics of the FLOURISHING Level

- **Mindset.** Fulfilled, content, and satisfied with their work and role; *I love what I do, and I love being part of this team.*
- **Posture/Attitude.** Approaches each day with joy and the desire to do their job with excellence and help others do the same; *what do you need and how can I best contribute to your life today?*
- **Relationships with Other Team Members.** Actively seeks relationships both inside and outside of work; seeks to help others be as successful or even more successful than they are; actively seeks to contribute to the lives of team members.
- **Work/Career.** Works diligently and successfully but demonstrates a healthy balance of working and living; understands that work is important, but not willing to sacrifice family, health, or time for work, at least not on a consistent basis.
- **Engagement.** Fully engaged in their job, seeking success for the team and the organization as a whole; while

advancement may be a desire, it is not all-consuming; a highly collaborative team player who cares little about who gets credit for the success of the team; comfortable and capable of leading but does not demand leadership.

- **Empathy.** Demonstrates care and concern for fellow team members; seeks to come alongside struggling or underperforming team members to help them in any way possible, but not do their work for them; when confrontation is needed, the conversation is kind and compassionate, while still being direct and focused; a proven listener and often one that fellow team members will seek out to discuss challenges—both personal and professional.
- **Empowerment.** Feels fully empowered to do own role; feels fully empowered to seek additional work or projects; holds team members accountable with patience and support; speaks up when given the opportunity to do so—especially when what is shared will help the team member, the team, or the organization be better.
- **Excellence.** Fully committed to excellence; a patient, confident leader who leads by example; when subpar performance is encountered, skillfully confronts and corrects what is necessary to prevent repeated failures; cares more for the success of the team and the organization than their own success.

Paul finished writing the section on *flourishing* and he thought, *I wonder who in our organization would be at the flourishing level?* "We need to make sure whoever is currently at that level is coaching and speaking into our team members' lives at Global Solutions," he wrote. "They have the mindset, the attitude, and the other characteristics that we want emulated throughout the organization. I wonder how we can 'clone' them?" Paul chuckled to himself as he wrote those words. "Our *flourishing* team members have found a home with us; they are satisfied and content," he continued. "They are contributors to our organization and not consumers. They invest in our team members. They are committed to learning and growing. They pitch in where needed, regardless of the task, project, or role. They are not concerned with titles, position, or doing something that is considered 'beneath them.' They don't care who gets the credit if the team wins. They don't care who is in charge if the leader is competent. They are willing to work when needed if they are not taken advantage of. They are positive influences."

> **What about you? What level—*diminishing, surviving, striving, thriving, flourishing*—would you say best describes the majority of the team members you work with? What level would you say best describes you right now? What characteristics do you observe in yourself that led you to choose that particular level? What would it take for you to move up a level?**

When we start rolling out training programs and processes, we need these team members teaching, facilitating, and coaching our other team members. They won't want to be perceived as a being put on a pedestal or elevated to "watch me" status; however, that is what we need to do, in essence, Paul thought. *Our* flourishing *team members are who we need to step up to have the greatest influence on Global Solution's culture. Our* flourishing *team members will help us build a* flourishing *organization!* Paul sat back in his chair, stretched his arms above his head, and smiled widely. He could hardly wait to get the team putting this together and rolling it out to the team as whole. He knew the process would not produce immediate results, but that was not the point. *We are playing for the next ten to twenty years, not the next one, two, or three*, he thought. *We are running a marathon here, maybe even an ultramarathon; however, I believe that years from now, we are going to look back on this time in our organization's history and view this as a watershed moment. This is a critical and exciting time for Global."* Paul was surprised by a sudden wave of emotion that came over him.

Paul had never been part of something like this in his career; it still didn't feel real to him, and he felt like he was in a fairy tale. In all his years working for other organizations, he had dreamt of working in a place like this, but he had all but given up hope that a place like Global existed. While he was caught up in the moment, he pulled out a "Thank You" card and wrote a brief but heartfelt note to Jude. In his short time at Global, he not only felt part of the team, but he also felt like he had found both a home and a second family. His wife noticed a difference in him, and his kids saw it as well. It wasn't a perfect place, and it wasn't without moments of stress, but no place is free of imperfections or stress. The difference Paul had experienced thus far was Jude's—and by extension the company's—overwhelming commitment to the team members, to the culture, and to relational health.

Paul finished his note to Jude, put it into an envelope, and sealed it. He made some additional notes in his notebook related to the process of identifying team members at each level but emphasized the need to discover the organization's *flourishing* team members. Paul then decided he needed to take a little break, but before he did, he made note of where he wanted to go next in his thinking and writing: *accelerators* and *barriers* to each level of the model.

The Flourishing Life Model. The Flourishing Life Model from an organizational perspective is now complete. Much more could have been written and many additional characteristics could have been added. The purpose was not to explore *every* characteristic or write a thesis on each of the characteristics; the purpose was to provide a few critical characteristics as succinctly as possible so any organization can adapt and adopt based on their culture, development, and circumstances. In Part III, we will explore practical exercises and implementation strategies that will allow any organization to adopt the principles and concepts we have been exploring on our journey.

The next chapter will examine the *accelerators* and the *barriers* to each of the levels. The purpose for examining these is to help identify the ways that organizations can help their team members overcome *barriers* and take advantage of *accelerators* for those that desire to move toward *flourishing* in their professional journeys. Let's jump into the *accelerators* and *barriers*!

CHAPTER 8

ACCELERATORS AND BARRIERS

Have you ever wanted to do something, and for whatever reason, it seemed like it just wasn't happening, no matter what you tried? Conversely, have you ever tried to do something, and it seemed like it went so much smoother and easier than you ever thought possible? This, at a high level, is what it is like when you experience *barriers* or *accelerators*. *Barriers* can prevent your team members from doing the things they really want to do, and *accelerators* can help propel your team members to be able to do what they really want to do.

The Flourishing Life Model has natural *accelerators* and *barriers* that accompany each level. We will be unpacking those characteristics that serve as *accelerators*—which help propel us on our journey to the next level; and those that serve as *barriers*—which can prevent us or slow us down on our journey to the next level.

Important Note: As with the characteristics listed for each level of the model, the list of *accelerators* and *barriers* for each of the levels is in no way an exhaustive list. The characteristics chosen for each are meant to serve as examples and as catalysts for your organizational evaluation. As you identify those *accelerators* and *barriers* in your team members' lives, ask these questions:

- If you identify an *accelerator*, how will you help your team members leverage that accelerator to help propel them forward on their journey?
- If you identify a *barrier*, what does your team member need to work on or seek help with to overcome or mitigate the *barrier,* so it doesn't slow them down or prevent them from moving forward on their journey?

It is important to note that not all the *accelerators* or *barriers* may be applicable for each level. The point is not to ensure that all apply; the point is to identify those that do apply. As with the characteristics we evaluated for each level, these are fluid—meaning what may currently be an *accelerator* or *barrier* may not have been such at a different stage of life or may not be in a future stage of life. Life is dynamic, and as a result, we experience life differently as we grow older and, hopefully, wiser.

Paul returned from his break, sat down, and got right to work.

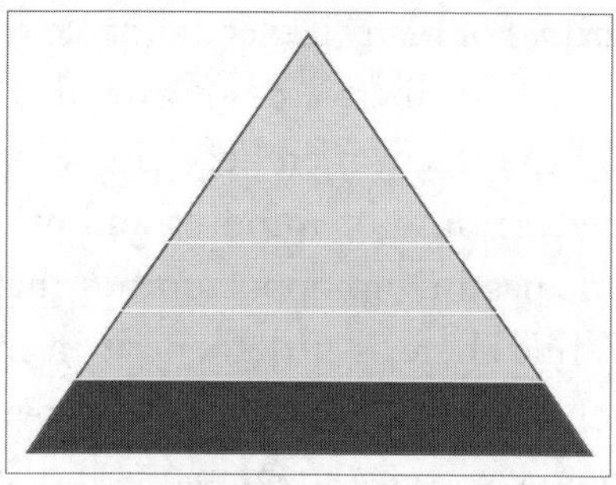

Accelerators and Barriers to DIMINISHING

Accelerators in the DIMINISHING Level

"What can help propel our team members from *diminishing* to the next level, *surviving*?" Paul began.

- **Belief.** When someone believes in someone else—even if it is just believing in the person's potential—it multiplies the same: *belief.* Team members operating at the *diminishing* level have lost hope and have given up believing in themselves and the organization. While belief alone will not automatically propel someone out of the *diminishing* mindset, it is a step. And while a step is not a journey, all journeys start by taking a first step.
- **Being Shown a Path.** Team members operating at the *diminishing* level have either lost hope that there is a path for them in the organization or they have stopped believing that a path exists for them. When a supervisor invests the time, energy, and resources necessary to help their team members see a path—specific to them—something magical emerges: *hope*. Those operating at the *diminishing* level have lost hope in either themselves or the organization; often it is both.

- **Opportunity.** For many understandable reasons, *diminishing*-level team members are not provided as many opportunities as other team members. Some of the reasons are self-inflicted because of mindset and attitude; other reasons include passing up opportunities that may have been offered. While there is little benefit in mandating that a team member takes an opportunity, providing the opportunity along with encouragement and coaching by the team member's supervisor can make the difference for a team member beginning their journey from *diminishing* versus a team member who remains stuck.

Paul paused for a moment. *Not every team member at the* diminishing *level will do what it takes to rise to the next level, no matter what we do as an organization to support them. What do we do then?* Paul pondered. "The unfortunate reality is that having zero turnover is not realistic, so it should not be a goal. If team members repeatedly refuse to change, grow, and take steps to move from *diminishing*, the harsh reality is that they will need the opportunity to succeed elsewhere," Paul wrote. "While it would be wonderful if everyone in our organization would aspire to be at the *flourishing* level, we will most likely never reach 100 percent of employees *flourishing*. And that is okay," Paul continued. "We will probably have team members at every level. The key for us is making sure that we are doing everything we can to provide the teaching, coaching, and training for every team member, so they can learn and grow. If our team members express a desire to learn and grow, and they remain teachable and coachable, we can work with any team member like that. It is when they become stubborn or immovable that we have a problem," Paul concluded. Then he moved on to the *barriers* in the *diminishing* level.

Barriers in the DIMINISHING Level

"What will keep our members at the *diminishing* level or prevent them from moving up to *surviving*?" Paul wrote.

- **Refusing to Engage.** It is possible to work with anyone who is teachable and coachable; however, if a team member refuses to engage—even after coaching and confrontation—there is little else that can be done. It is akin to the adage "You can lead a horse to water, but you cannot make them drink."
- **Choosing to NOT Learn, Grow, or Try.** When a team member is presented with opportunities to learn, grow, and become a better version of themselves, but refuses to cooperate, listen, or even try, there is little else we can present to help them.
- **Not Responding to Coaching.** Being unresponsive to coaching is consistent with the other two barriers to growing from *diminishing* to *surviving*. If a team member does not respond to one-on-one coaching by their supervisor or even external coaching, then it seems pointless to try to motivate someone to become an engaged and contributing member of the team when that is not what they want to do.

As Paul contemplated the *barriers* in the *diminishing* level, he came to a grim, yet realistic, conclusion. "If a team member is in the *diminishing* level and refuses to engage; chooses to not learn, grow, or even try; and does not respond to coaching, then there is only one option that remains," Paul said aloud as he wrote. "That individual can no longer be part of the Global Solutions team. Furthermore," he added, "these team members must be identified immediately because they are potentially toxic to the culture of the organization. These people are the classic 'naysayers,' and having 'naysayers' as part of the organization who are not willing to change is unacceptable. If they are not dealt with—immediately—their attitude and their behavior will spread like wildfire." Paul then continued, "Whenever negative attitudes or behaviors contrary to our desired culture are tolerated and not confronted, they are actually endorsed and blessed. This absolutely must not be the case at Global Solutions if we are going to have a culture that is healthy, engaged, and flourishing."

Paul leaned back in his chair and began thinking of his interactions with the team members at Global Solutions thus far. He asked himself if anyone he had met was currently at this stage, *diminishing* with no desire to change, grow, or try. He made some more notes in his notebook to discuss with Emma on Monday, although he was beginning to realize that the amount of notes he had added to discuss with Emma was turning into either an all-day type of meeting or multiple meetings. He was okay with that thought, however, because what they were working on was foundational for the next ten to twenty years in the life of Global Solutions.

Paul then turned back to his computer and moved on to the *accelerators* and *barriers* to *surviving.*

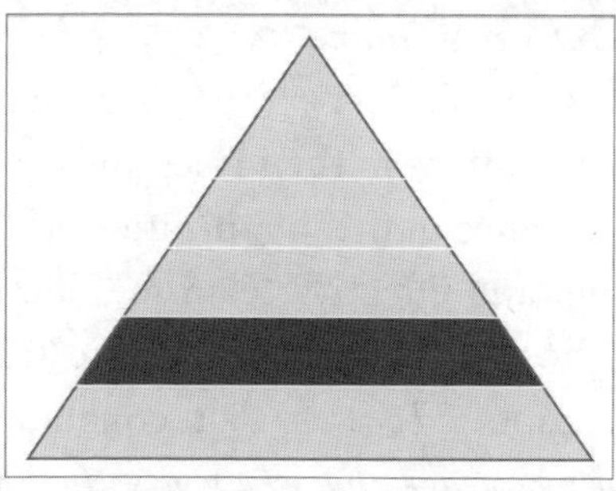

Accelerators and Barriers to SURVIVING

Accelerators in the SURVIVING Level

"What can help propel our team members from *surviving* to the next level, *striving*?" Paul wrote. "Without using clichés or simple formulaic answers, *accelerators* to move from *surviving* to *striving* usually mean that something must break—the way of doing things must stop working. It is too easy to stay at the *surviving* level without a catalyst that makes our team members realize that something is just not working." Then, he moved on to defining the *accelerators* in the *surviving* level.

- **Status Quo Becomes Untenable.** When does change become necessary? When the way things have "always have been done" stops working—or at least stops working as well as it once did. For some team members and some personality types, the status quo is not only preferred but also actively pursued. *For those team members who do not seek to change their situation or alter the status quo, is that okay?* Paul wondered. There is always work that needs to be done that is routine, predictable, and necessary—especially as organizations grow and expand. *If we have team members who are content and satisfied in routine, predictable,* *and stable roles day in and day out, is that okay for Global Solutions? I think the answer is yes*, he thought. When team members are content in their roles and they do not seek to change or advance in the organization, if they are healthy, contributing, and effective team members, then we have needs for those roles and want those team members in the organization. *The issue*, Paul concluded, *is when team members acknowledge that the ways they have done things no longer work and they want a change. These are the team members we must identify, come alongside, coach, and provide opportunities for them to learn, grow, and advance.*

- **Growing in Emotional Intelligence.** As team members grow in their ability to understand self and others, it creates opportunities for leadership. The main reason this occurs is because effective leaders must be able to understand both their individual strengths and weaknesses and their team members' strengths and weaknesses to effectively communicate, delegate, coach, grow, and hold accountable. Leaders who lack emotional intelligence struggle with relationship building and relational interactions, which are crucial to effectively leading other people—especially in team settings.
- **Courage to Take Risks.** Moving from the *surviving* level requires not just wanting to improve but also the desire to take on a certain amount of risk. At the *surviving* level, often the survivor knows what it takes to be able to survive on a day-to-day basis; they have not only gotten proficient at it, but they have also come to rely and depend upon it. When a team member begins to acknowledge that the ways they have been doing things are no longer working, they are also admitting that they are unsure—or less

sure—of what to do next. Hence, risk enters the equation. Paul wrote, "When a team member arrives at this point, we have to be the best we can possibly be to provide a low-risk opportunity for this team member to begin to spread their wings." Too often, it seems, a team member takes a risk of asking for an opportunity or a greater challenge, and the supervisor does one of three things: (1) gives them something that needs to be done but has been delayed and passed around because nobody wants to do it; (2) gives them something that is way above the team member's ability to successfully accomplish, like something that is ten steps more challenging instead of one step, for instance; or (3) the supervisor does not take the person seriously and either blows off the request or just adds more tasks and projects to make the team member "busier."

As Paul finished writing the *accelerators* in the *surviving* level, he thought, *When a team member seeks to grow, change, and rise from* surviving, *we must provide support, coaching, and resources so they have every opportunity to succeed.* Again, Paul made some sidenotes in his notebook before moving to *barriers* to *surviving.*

Barriers to SURVIVING

"What will keep our members at the *surviving* level or prevent them from moving up to *striving*?" Paul wrote.

- **Status Quo Is Acceptable.** When a team member is content and satisfied in their role, and they are a healthy, engaged team member, then the status quo is okay. As stated, every organization has routine, predictable, stable roles that do roughly the same thing day to day. Some team members are content in those roles, and they are necessary roles that serve vital functions in the organization. If those team members are truly satisfied, engaged, and contributory team members, we need them and they need us. The problem comes when the status quo becomes no longer acceptable; this requires action on the part of the company.

- **Lack of Desire to Change.** A lack of desire to change is a different issue than accepting the status quo. As organizations grow and expand, change becomes not only inevitable but also necessary. Team members must be willing to grow, adapt, and change with the ever-demanding fluctuations that both time and expansion bring. If a team member is reluctant to change—or worse, is openly hostile to change—their unwillingness must be addressed immediately. It is difficult enough as it is to keep up with the changes facing organizations every day: existing competition, new competition, technology, regulations, cultural shifts, and political changes, to name just a few. When a team member digs in, refuses to change, and stubbornly resists necessary organizational changes, that team member may not be able to remain a member in that organization.

- **Comfort**. Some personality types are concerned with comfort—namely their own—above anything else. Resistance to change can present issues when changes are inevitably implemented. Change is uncomfortable; even good change is uncomfortable. Change, even when it is necessary, has an element of the unknown that can be unsettling for anyone. However, what is unsettling for some is nearly debilitating for those whose own comfort is a primary motivation.

Paul finished the section on *barriers* in *surviving* and leaned back in his chair. *The key to having team members at the* surviving *level is to make sure that their "surviving" is not causing others to be more diminished in their roles*, he thought. *Organizational life and culture are difficult enough as it is; however, just like the barriers in the* diminishing *level, when a team member is stubbornly resistant to change because it makes them uncomfortable or it isn't what they want, we must address this head-on when we know it and observe it. If we don't, then we are sending the message that this kind of behavior is not only tolerated but also encouraged, and we just cannot afford to have that at Global Solutions.* Paul wrapped up his thinking, made some additional notes in his notebook, and then turned his attention to the *accelerators* and *barriers* to *striving*.

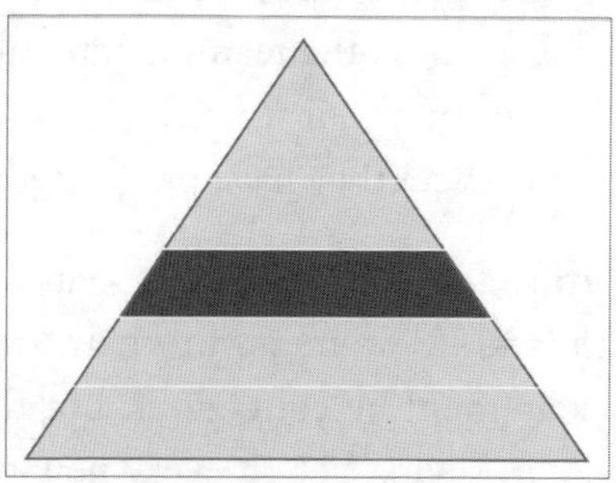

Accelerators and Barriers to STRIVING

Accelerators in the STRIVING Level

"What can help propel our team members from *striving* to the next level, *thriving*?" Paul wrote.

- **Vision for What Can Be.** When a team member starts their journey from *striving* to *thriving*, the catalyst is often gaining a vision for what they can be—professionally, personally, or both. This vision can be found within the person when the person imagines what they can become. Or a supervisor, colleague, or family member can provide the vision. Often this happens when someone observes something in the other person that reveals a spark of ingenuity, uncovers a passion, or identifies a gifting or calling. When this happens, the reaction around the team member is often akin to "Where did that come from?" Or maybe "I didn't know you could do that, or that you were passionate about that." When those sparks are identified, the best thing for that team member is encouragement to explore it more fully and deeply. The exciting possibility is that the team member may be on the leading edge of discovering what it is that would propel them to the *flourishing* level. The risk at this level is that the moment may pass without recognition or acknowledgement, which can cause the team member to be reluctant to continue their journey—or worse, start to migrate backward from the point where they have progressed.

- **Concentration of Effort.** As a team member gains momentum and excitement in their *striving,* not only can their excitement be contagious, but they may also get carried away in saying yes to every new opportunity they identify or that comes their way. Saying yes is a double-edged sword. On one side, it is great when you have a team member who is willing to pitch in and help; on the other side, they may not know their capacity and limitations, which can lead to being stretched too thin. When team members are stretched too thin, then everything they do suffers—not just the new things they committed to. The key, when a team member is excitedly in the *striving* level, is to help the team member identify, as quickly as possible, what they are passionate about and good at doing. Then, help the team member evaluate what they should say yes to, but even more importantly, what they should say no to. The key to accomplishment is the concentration of effort.

- **Eliminating Paper Walls.** What are paper walls? Paper walls are walls, barriers, and limitations that exist only in one's mind; they do not actually exist. The difference between moving up to *thriving* or back to *surviving* is realizing that paper walls are not real. Too often, a team member may say they are not equipped or prepared for something because of insecurity, experience, trauma, or harsh or unfair feedback. It is way too easy to personalize failure rather than separating it out as an event. If a team member seemingly has an issue with "paper walls," helping them push through their paper walls will help them change and grow not only professionally but also personally.

As Paul finished writing, he thought, *If we can identify and come alongside our* striving *team members, they are the future* thriving *leaders for Global Solutions. Not only that, but they are also our potential* flourishing *team members. We can help them grow into healthy, engaged team members with their eyes on* flourishing, *not just* thriving. He made a few notes in his notebook and then jumped right into the *barriers* at the *striving* level.

Barriers in the STRIVING Level

"What will keep our members at the *striving* level or prevent them from moving up to *thriving*?" Paul wrote.

- **Lack of Knowledge, Training, or Skill.** If a team member has the desire to learn, grow, and take on more responsibility, but they lack the knowledge, training, or skill, it is up to the organization to provide access to that knowledge, training, and/or skill. If the organization does not make it available, then we will most likely lose valuable team members because they will become frustrated and deflated. The key is to understand the gap. If the gap is based on desire or attitude, the organization cannot do much with that because that is internal to the person; however, if the gap is knowledge, training, or skill, the organization can—and probably should—work to close that gap.

- **Lack of Desire.** Desire is an internally driven motivation. If a team member does not have the desire to learn, grow, or advance, there is little the organization can do to help. Team members with a lack of motivation and desire must either find a role in which they can perform with excellence day to day, or find another organization where they can succeed.
- **Fear of Failure.** The fear of failure is a different animal. Fear of failure may be justified or unjustified; either way, it is a real emotion that people experience. If the fear of failure is identified in team members as a *barrier* for progressing toward the *thriving* level, the organization has a handful of options to consider. First, would there be a way to give a small opportunity that would help restore some confidence in the team member? Second, is there a possibility of offering to cover the cost of counseling? Third, would coaching be an opportunity—either internally or externally, at no cost to the team member? Fourth, is there another leader in the organization the team member could "shadow" for a period—ideally someone who has wrestled

with the same core fears? There are undoubtedly other options. These are just a few options to consider helping our *striving* team members not get stuck in their current journey nor slide down a level.

As Paul finished, he sat back and thought, *Of all the levels, we are at the greatest risk of losing our* striving *team members. Maybe I am off, but it makes sense to me.* He pondered further. *Our* striving *team members are motivated, they caught a glimpse of what could be, and they are moving quickly. They want to learn, grow, change, and take on more. They are eager. They may not always know what they are eager for, but they are eager. Once we identify a* striving *team member, we must figure out a path for them, or we will most likely lose them. They are searching for and desiring a path forward*, Paul concluded. *If we do not provide one for them, they will find a path at a different organization, which is only fine if that is what we really want them to do.* Paul reached over and made some additional notes in his now famous notebook before jumping into the *accelerators* and *barriers* in the *thriving* level.

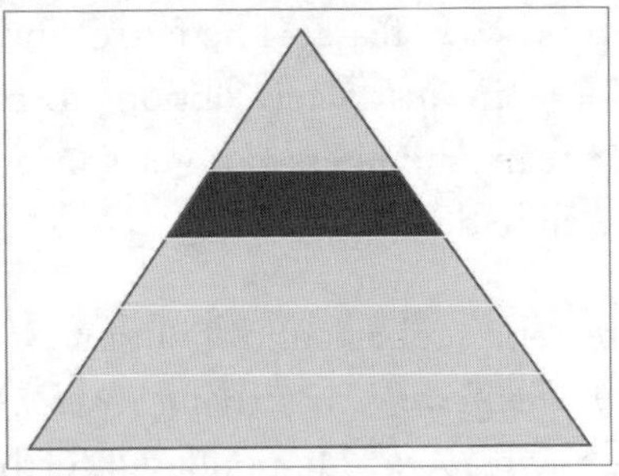

Accelerators and Barriers to THRIVING

Accelerators in the THRIVING Level

"What can help propel our team members from *thriving* to the next level, *flourishing*?" Paul wrote.

- **Demonstrated Humility.** *Demonstrated humility sounds like an oxymoron. If someone is humble, isn't it just known and seen? Why does it have to be demonstrated?* Paul wondered as he wrote the definition of *demonstrated humility. Demonstrated humility* means a proven track record over time of putting others over self, of accepting one's need for God and others, and of realizing that the world does not revolve around self. *Demonstrated humility* means being committed to the greater good over individual preference; it means a growing awareness of self—specifically the aspects of the impact of one's own words, attitudes, and behaviors on the people around them. And it means the willingness to flow and flex in and out of the spotlight when necessary. It can be difficult for someone at the *thriving* level to be willing to take a back seat or step out of the spotlight—especially if or when they feel like they have earned or deserve it; however, when a *thriving* team member willingly steps aside and then intentionally supports someone else in their growth journey, it sends a powerful message to the rest of the team.

- **LOITSD (Long Obedience in the Same Direction).** Often attributed to the prophet Nehemiah in the Old Testament of the Bible, *long obedience in the same direction* means being committed to something—a vision, a mission, a belief, a calling, a dream, a purpose—over the long haul, even in the face of adversity. Perhaps it would be better stated as *especially in the face of adversity!* When the prophet Nehemiah visited Jerusalem for the first time and saw the city in near ruins, with the wall around the city in complete destruction, two things happened to him: (1) his heart broke within him, and (2) his calling was cemented. Nehemiah returned to his homeland and over the course of time, petitioned King Artaxerxes to grant him men, money, and other resources to rebuild the wall around Jerusalem. Because of Nehemiah's persistent obedience to his calling, not only was the wall rebuilt, but it was rebuilt in a time frame no one thought possible and with fewer resources than anyone imagined. Nehemiah's *long obedience in the same direction* not only rebuilt the wall around Jerusalem, but it saved countless lives as the city was once again protected from outside forces that sought to destroy both the city and the people within it.

  LOITSD applies today in much the same way. When someone is committed to what they believe in and they obediently pursue it over the long term, three things tend to happen over time: (1) opportunities open that most likely would not have opened without persistent obedience; (2) respect and admiration from others often arise from seeing one's passionate, long-term pursuit of a dream or calling; and (3) proficiency and efficiency are gained from the daily practice and engagement in that which one passionately pursues day in and day out. The temptation from many at the *thriving* level is to drift into the mindset of "maximizing one's economic potential." In other words, taking the expertise, proficiency, and efficiency of one's skills and abilities, and then shopping them to the highest bidder. While this may yield more compensation over one's lifetime, it rarely yields more satisfaction, sense of purpose, or increased meaning in life. This does not suggest that someone who has become extremely talented at their job should settle for compensation at a level much below the market rate, but it does suggest that moving frequently from organization to organization to increase one's compensation becomes an exercise in futility—at least if the pursuit of long-term satisfaction, purpose, meaning, and joy are important. This means that organizations must do the best they can to provide competitive compensation packages to their top-performing team members, or they will risk losing them; however, at some point, the discussion is no longer about the amount of compensation. Too often, team members at the *thriving* level attribute their level of compensation to their level of individual worth. This is often tied deeply to one's self-perception and identity. Those who realize and accept that their identity and worth has nothing to do with the size of their compensation package have an opportunity to transcend to the *flourishing* level. On the other hand, those who equate their level of compensation to identity and self-worth will have a more difficult journey to the *flourishing* level.

- **Team over Individual.** Team members at the *thriving* level are usually wonderful individual contributors. They often rise to the top, so to speak, by their abilities to get things done predictably and repeatably with excellent results. The reality is that in any organization, no one person performs on his or her own; it is always a team effort. There are team members who excel and rise to the top in every organization. These are usually the *thriving* team members who get excellent results and are compensated for their abilities to get things done in an excellent fashion. Those team members who realize it was a team working together, not their efforts alone, that brought success are on the journey toward *flourishing*. When a team member is convinced it is their efforts alone that brought them success, it is extremely difficult to move beyond the *thriving* level.

Wow! This is some powerful stuff, Paul contemplated as he finished the accelerators in the thriving level. *Humility, long obedience in the same direction, and team over self. If our team members get this—and live this—it will not only change our organization, but it will also change their lives.* He sat back with a sudden realization. *This will change my life,* he thought. *Am I living these? I believe these are all true, but am I really living these? If I had to be gut-level honest right now, I am not. I have been so focused on myself for most of my career: my happiness, my fulfillment, my position, what is fair to me, what is owed to me.* Paul continued to ponder his approach to his career—his mindset, his thinking, his behaviors, his attitudes. The longer he sat there, the more somber he became. *I have been living in a jail cell of my own making. I built this jail cell, I chose to live in it, and I have been holding the key the entire time! I could have chosen to open the door, walk out, and be free. But no, I had to stay in that cell by choosing a victim's mindset, choosing to believe I was owed something, and believing I was entitled to more and better.* "What a fool I have been." Paul whispered those final six words to himself as he wiped away tears that flowed freely as he stayed deep in thought. *I know. I just know that we have team members at Global who are in similar prisons of their own making. And I bet they feel like I have felt for years: that there is no other way, or there is no way out—if they are even aware of the prison cell they are in*, he thought. "Whenever possible, I need to share my story with them. I need to let them know there is hope!" A smile returned to Paul's face as he wrote the word "hope" in his last sentence.

As before, Paul made some notes in his notebook and then immediately jumped into the barriers in the thriving level.

Barriers in the THRIVING Level

"What will keep our members at the *thriving* level or prevent them from moving up to *flourishing*?" Paul wrote.

- **Comfort.** Comfort in the sense of a *barrier* has little to do with feeling comfortable—as in settling into your favorite chair at night, in front of a roaring fire, and a glass of your favorite wine or bourbon in your hand. Hopefully everyone can feel that kind of comfort from time to time. The kind of *comfort* that will prevent a team member from moving from *thriving* to *flourishing* has to do with not wanting to change what has been working or has gotten the person to where they are. It can be scary to think about changing what has been working, much less actually *doing* something about it. While being content is desirable for everyone regardless of the level they are at currently, being "comfortable" means wanting to stick with what is known, what works, and what is predictable. Moving from *thriving* to *flourishing* often means venturing into the unknown, which can be unsettling. There is nothing inherently wrong with wanting to be, or to stay, comfortable; this is not a moral issue. However, if someone desires to move to *flourishing*, then this will most likely mean being uncomfortable for a season, and that season may be short—or long.

- **Something to Prove, Lose, or Hide.** Whenever someone lives in the tension of having something to prove, lose, or hide, they are usually motivated to accomplish, succeed, and thrive beyond what some may consider "normal." There is often a deep-rooted insecurity and fear that drives people who live in this tension. They often fear things such as the following:
  - "I am not enough."
  - "I have to prove my worth."
  - "I may lose everything."
  - "I don't measure up."
  - "I am not like ______ [fill in the blank with another person's name]."
  - "What if I am found out?"
  - "I hope no one ever sees behind the mask."
  - "I am just faking it."

Team members who live with something to prove, lose, or hide will spend time, energy, and resources trying to outlive the shadows they are "boxing" or the shadows of their past that are "haunting" them. If someone stays in this mode, it will be difficult for them to focus on the critical factors of *flourishing* because they will be consumed with the factors related to *thriving*. It is one thing if a person intentionally remains at the *thriving* level because that is what they have chosen to do; however, when someone is in the mode of "something to prove, lose, or hide," they are often unaware that another path—another journey—is available to them.

- **Pride.** Pride is such an interesting word. Parents are "proud" of their kids, and that is a good thing. Students and workers are "proud" of the work they have done, and that is a good thing. We take "pride" in our country of origin or our family heritage, and those are good things. If these forms of pride are good, healthy, and encouraged, then what is wrong with personal pride? Pride that is rooted in self-aggrandizement, arrogance, and selfishness is unhealthy, damaging, and toxic; it is the kind of pride that leads to false confidence and thoughts such as these:
    - "I did this on my own, by myself, with no one else."
    - "I am better than anyone else."
    - "I am great; everyone else is beneath me."
    - "I can do anything I set my mind to doing, without anyone's help."
    - "I am amazing; I don't care what anyone else thinks."

People who are filled with pride do not acknowledge their need for God or for others. They are usually unwilling to be confronted or corrected, do not wish to receive coaching or feedback, and rarely—if ever—think they are wrong or in error. Pride leads to haughtiness and, ultimately, to destruction. Proverbs 16:18 says, "Pride goes before destruction, and a haughty spirit before a fall."[15] When people struggle with pride, they often push people away—not necessarily intentionally but unintentionally, because their communication, both verbal and nonverbal, is that they don't need anyone. Team members who struggle with pride often have achieved success and are very gifted at what they do; many of them have been elevated several times through the organization or have risen quickly through the ranks. To make the move from *thriving* to *flourishing* would mean facing and dealing with one's pride head-on by acknowledging, at minimum, one's need for the team, and ideally, one's need for God.

Paul sat back from his computer and breathed a loud sigh. "This was a difficult section. I see all of these barriers in myself, at least to some degree." Paul said. "I am driven and motivated by many of these. I want to prove that I am somebody—somebody worthy of following. I feel like I have a lot to prove! One of my best friends has entrusted one of the most important aspects of his organization to me—the culture and development of the people. I feel like I have everything to lose, especially if I mess this up." *I love to be comfortable*, Paul thought, *and I know I can be prideful at times. Wow, this section was like taking a hard look in the mirror. This is some difficult stuff. I need a break.* Paul stood up from his chair. It was well into the afternoon now, so

[15] Proverbs 16:18 (NKJV).

he went to the kitchen, took out an ice-cold IPA, and poured himself a glass. He refilled his glass of water as well. He stood in the kitchen for a moment reflecting as he drank half his beer. He then slowly shuffled back into his study to take a seat at his desk once again.

Paul made a few notes before returning to his keyboard to jump into the *accelerators* and *barriers* to *flourishing.*

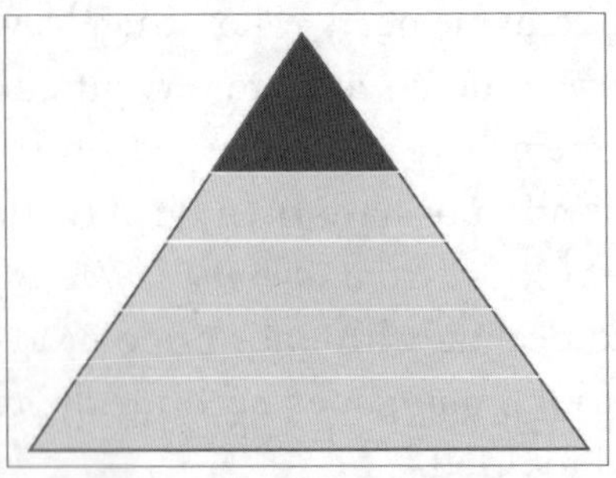

Accelerators and Barriers to FLOURISHING

Accelerators in the FLOURISHING Level

"What can help keep our team members focused on *flourishing*?" Paul wrote.

- **Having a Culture That Encourages and Rewards *Flourishing*.** Eric Liddell made a profound statement in the movie *Chariots of Fire*. He said, "In the dust of defeat as well as the laurels of victory, there is a glory to be found if one has done his best. God made me fast. And when I run, I feel His pleasure."[16] *What does it mean to feel* God's

[16] *Chariots of Fire.*

pleasure? Paul pondered. *What does it mean to feel* pleasure *from another person—a boss, a coworker, a parent, a spouse, a sibling, a friend?* Feeling the pleasure of someone else may seem like an ethereal concept to get your mind around; however, experiencing the pleasure of someone else—God included—is something that seems to be universally desired and longed for.

What about you? When was the last time you felt the pleasure of someone else—or felt that someone was pleased with you? When did you last express your pleasure with someone else? Don't wait any longer; express your pleasure to someone in your life today!

"If having an organizational culture where team members *flourish* is of paramount importance for Global, then the structures—especially compensation, reward, and advancement structures—must be aligned to that importance," Paul wrote. "We need to build our culture so that our people feel the pleasure of those they work with—and for—as they perform their jobs day in and day out, not just when they achieve something extraordinary," Paul stated emphatically as he typed. "We need to take time to celebrate the wins and victories, but we also need to make sure we are communicating pleasure for the mundane daily tasks, projects, and functions necessary for the organization to run efficiently and effectively."

Building a *flourishing* organization means having the infrastructure, processes, and procedures in place that are aligned to building *flourishing* individuals. This means ensuring that reward systems and what is celebrated—as well as what isn't—aligns to the core values espoused by the organization.

- **Adopting the Mindset: "It Is Not about Me."** Living and staying at the *flourishing* level means accepting that life is bigger than you. Furthermore, it means accepting that the world does not revolve around you, nor is everything about you. When someone adopts the mindset that everything is about them or the world revolves around them, it is difficult to get that person to see the perspective of others; it is also difficult for them to think about how their behaviors, attitudes, and actions affect those around them. Adopting the mindset that "it is not about me," means that you are growing in self- and others-awareness to better understand how you affect others around you. With growing self- and others-awareness comes the opportunity to have greater influence and impact in the lives of the people you are with daily—whether at work, at home, at worship, or in the community. In addition to completing personality assessments, two terrific books that address growing in self- and others-awareness are *The Man in the Mirror*[17] and *TrueFaced.*[18] Inside of organizations, adopting the mindset of "it is not about me" means being aware that teams are comprised of multiple people with various perspectives, opinions, preferences, likes, dislikes, and personalities; it means showing deference and prioritizing others' needs above your own.

---

[17] Patrick Morley, *The Man in the Mirror* (Nashville: Zondervan, 2014).
[18] Bill Thrall, Bruce McNicol, and John S. Lynch, *TrueFaced* (Colorado Springs: NavPress, 2004).

- **Focusing on Legacy, Not Immediacy.** Staying at the *flourishing* level means maintaining the perspective that life is wild, precious, and short; it truly is more meaningful to give than receive. Living with the end in mind—focusing on what you want your life to be remembered for when your journey concludes—means aligning your focus and living now so the trajectory of your life's journey matches your desired legacy at the end. The *thriving* level focuses more on the here and now, immediate reward, or current pleasure rather than delayed gratification; none of this is inherently wrong or bad—not in a moral sense, anyway. When individuals make decisions for current pleasure or reward without regard for the future, they often sacrifice future reward for present satisfaction—even when the future reward has the potential to be much more fulfilling or meaningful. Focusing on legacy often means choosing to delay reward, make sacrifices in the present, or be extra diligent in ensuring that decisions align with your desired end-of-life focus. In organizational life, focusing on legacy over immediacy means making decisions that are strategic and long term in nature, and not tactical and short term. Choices are not dichotomous—all or nothing—a balance is always required between long and short term. Legacy mindset means investing in people, leadership development, and a *flourishing* culture are prioritized over maximizing economic gains and financial returns. This does not mean that organizations should not seek to optimize operations, but it does mean that the emphasis on generating financial returns is not prioritized over the investment in the organization's most important asset: *its people*. Too many organizations give lip service that its people are their most important assets, but then make strategic and tactical decisions that communicate that maximizing financial returns is the primary focus of the organization. Focusing on legacy means aligning the strategic and tactical decisions of the organization with the stated and espoused values of the organization.

As Paul finished the section on *accelerators* in the *flourishing* level, he read over what he had written. *I need to have a conversation with Jude about this as soon as possible*, he thought. *If we are truly serious about building a flourishing organization, we must make sure that our policies, procedures, structures, and strategic decision-making are aligned to what we espouse and aspire to build at Global.* Paul sent a quick email to Jude and asked if they could grab breakfast or lunch in the upcoming week or two. Paul then turned his focus to working on the *barriers* in the *flourishing* level.

Barriers in the FLOURISHING Level

"What can keep our members from staying at the *flourishing* level?" Paul wrote.

- **Mission Drift.** The book *Mission Drift*[19] presents a compelling case and practical exercises for keeping an organization on mission over the long term. One of the primary responsibilities of organizational leadership—especially the senior leaders such as owners, CEOs, presidents, executive directors, superintendents, senior pastors, or boards of directors—is to safeguard, communicate frequently, and proliferate the vision, mission, and purpose of the

[19] Greer and Horst, *Mission Drift.*

organization. Leaders are responsible and need to be held accountable for keeping the organization on course and on mission. Organizations drift from their mission when the leadership of the organization does one of three things. First, they do not protect the original intent of the founders of the organization. Second, they intentionally change the vision, mission, and purpose of the organization. Third, they tolerate and permit behaviors and attitudes that are contrary to the stated and aspirational values of the organization. The natural progression in organizations is to drift away from the original intent; it takes proactivity and intentionality to keep an organization on mission.

- **Fear.** Fear is a powerful motivator, and it can also be a barrier in our lives. Fear can move us to action to accomplish feats that have no logical explanation. But fear can also render us immobile, paralyzed, and sitting in a corner sucking our fingers, wishing that the big, bad monsters would go away. One of the common characteristics of *thriving* is success—monetary, career, position, title, and so forth. Moving to *flourishing* often means intentionally deciding to change one's focus or path in life. The *thriving* path often means greater success as defined by having *more* and *better* things. The *flourishing* path often means greater purpose, meaning, fulfillment, and satisfaction but may actually lead to *fewer* things. Although the concept of experiencing the *flourishing* life may sound attractive and seem like an amazing experience, the fear of the unknown and the fear of blazing a new path may be too great for some to stay on the *flourishing* journey. It is not *if* fear will creep in but *when*. Organizations that are serious about building a flourishing culture must proactively address these fears by reassuring those on the journey that they are seen and supported.

- **Rewarding Contrary Behaviors and Attitudes.** Occasionally, organizations reward behaviors and attitudes that are contrary to the desired and aspirational behaviors and attitudes of the organizational culture. When that happens, there is an unsustainable system in place. If those errant reward systems are not corrected, the organization will never realize its aspirational behaviors, attitudes, and values. Reward systems must be put in place that recognize, encourage, and reward that which is important to the organization. Too often, organizations have wonderful aspirational values but get frustrated when those values are not practiced or realized. When the organization reviews the underlying systems, processes, and procedures of the reward systems in place, the reasons as to why those values are not realized become painfully clear. In actuality, those systems reward the values *opposite* of those the organization is aspiring to. It is critical to examine the systems (e.g., reward systems, correction processes, performance optimization procedures, etc.) in place to ensure full alignment to the aspirational values of the organization. If misalignment exists, the possibility of achieving the aspirational values becomes a monumental task that often results in frustration, discouragement, and confusion. In turn, those negative results often translate into higher turnover, lower morale, and less engagement from those team members who remain.

Paul finished his final section and breathed a loud sigh. "This is good stuff—heavy and difficult in places—but good stuff. Writing this down, unfortunately, is the easy part. Now what about practicing and implementing everything? That is going to be the difficult part. We have a huge opportunity and an enormous responsibility ahead. I am excited, overwhelmed, and intimidated—all at the same time!" Paul told himself out loud. Then, with a sudden realization, he stood and exclaimed, "But I am not alone in this! I have Jude's full support, I have my team, and I have the other executives who are *fully*—not marginally—on board with this."

What about you? What barriers and accelerators do you identify in the lives of your team members? What barriers and accelerators do you identify in your own life? What can you do now to begin to overcome your barriers and utilize accelerators to become healthier, more engaged, and more productive?

Paul decided to go for a walk after sitting in his chair nearly all day. He needed to stretch his legs, get some exercise, and clear his head. As he walked and sometimes ran, he enjoyed the crisp, fresh air in his lungs and the warm sun on his face on a chilly afternoon. As Paul reflected on his day of writing, he smiled at times without thinking. Other times, he pursed his lips, thinking of how critically important this time was for the future of Global Solutions. Paul lost track of time and space as he walked and thought. He made his way back home after what he thought was a fifteen-minute walk, only to realize he had actually been walking for forty-five minutes.

As he made his way up the driveway, he noticed Patty's car. Walking in through the kitchen door, Patty was in the kitchen, drinking a glass of water. "How was your day, babe?" Paul asked.

"It was a good day. We had a great time together. How was yours?" Patty asked.

"This may sound weird," Paul answered, "but I spent all day at my computer, working on documenting all the conversations from this week and clearing my head. I went out for a walk to get some exercise, which is where I just was."

"You worked all day?" Patty asked, bewildered. "Is that what you wanted to do?"

"Honey, this may seem crazy, but I had one of most invigorating days I've had in a long time," Paul said. "What I did today is going to not only make a difference in our team members' lives, but it will also change lives. I'm so excited to start training, practicing, and implementing what we're working on. We have a real opportunity to build something special at Global—*flourishing individuals building a flourishing organization.*"

"Well, I don't understand everything you just said, but I'm thrilled you're so excited. I haven't seen you this enthusiastic in years." Patty's voice trailed off as tears came to her eyes.

Paul embraced Patty for a few minutes. They decided to make dinner together and have a movie night as a family. As Paul was watching the movie, his mind drifted for a few minutes to what he needed to do next. He knew he needed another day of writing to document the integration and implementation plan of what he had put together thus far. Before they went to bed, he mentioned to Patty that he needed another day to finish up. She asked if he could work from home one day in the upcoming week. Paul thought about it for a minute and said that he may be able to get away on Wednesday of the upcoming week. As he laid his head down on his pillow, a smile came to his face, and then he fell fast asleep.

This concludes Part II of our journey. As we continue to follow Paul's journey at Global, we are also learning along the way what it takes to build flourishing organizations. Before we move into Part III, let's quickly review. We started our journey by looking at examples of engaged and flourishing teams. We then moved into the "un-formula" formula of engaged, flourishing teams. We stopped at empathy and spent time learning about its importance. Next, we made a stop at empowerment and learned the lessons that are critical to empowering individuals within the organization. Finally, we made a stop at excellence where we learned about the importance of having an unwavering commitment to excellence in all things.

Paul then took us to the organizational adaptation of the Flourishing Life Model, where he walked us through each of the five levels. We just completed our walk through the *accelerators* and *barriers* of each level of the model. Finally, we will learn how to integrate what we have covered into practical, implementable exercises, constructs, and processes to equip you to build flourishing organizations.

Part III will continue to follow Paul's journey in Global Solutions through Paul developing practical and implementable exercises for Global. As with any concept, the power of a concept is not in defining it; it is in the application and implementation of it. The last thing that Global or any organization needs is another book of concepts and ideas that are not practical or implementable. The focus of Part III is providing practical solutions to complex problems that every organization faces. People issues in organizations are simultaneously the most complex and most important. Therefore, providing practical solutions to complex people problems can have significant impact in the lives of people, which provides significant impact in the life of the organization.

Are you excited to continue our journey into Part III and begin implementing solutions? I am! Let's go.

PART III

CHAPTER 9

INTEGRATION: EMPATHY

Have you ever read something—whether a book, newspaper article, or blog—that captured your imagination, made you think, and left you leaning in and wanting more, and then… that was it? No more information, no integration, no "this is where you go for further information," or "this is how you get it done." Hopefully, since you have come this far on our journey together, you are willing to travel a little further.

This book is not just a nice story or good concepts that make you think; hopefully, both are true for you as you have read to this point, however. This book is also a reflection of life (although the names of characters and organizations have been changed) and what can happen when organizations, and especially organizational leaders, get serious and intentional about building healthy organizational culture. *Well, that is just great*, you may be thinking. *Now what do I do with all of this?* As I promised, this book will not leave you hanging. In the final leg of our journey, we will be laser-focused on integration and application. If one or more concepts from this book have piqued your interest and you are asking yourself, *Now what?* then Part III is for you.

Paul is about to transition his thinking from conceptual development into the integration of these concepts in the day-to-day world at Global Solutions. Paul will introduce us to several examples, practices, exercises, and processes that are simple to understand, relevant, and implementable. You may only be interested in some, or in specific parts, of what you have read so far, and that is okay; however, everything we covered on our journey through this book is available to you in Part III so you can implement solutions in your own organization, if you so desire.

Without further ado, let's return to Paul's story.

Paul returned to work on Monday with an extra bounce in his step and excitement in his spirit. Even though he had spent all day Saturday working, he was energized, recharged, and ready to go. Paul was excited to be at work! As he was walking to his office first thing that morning, he ran into Jude. "Hey bud, how was your weekend?" Jude asked.

"It was fantastic, Jude! Thank you for asking. How was yours?"

"Mine was very good. Anything special happen this weekend that made your weekend so 'fantastic'?" Jude inquired.

"I had the day to myself on Saturday, Jude. I worked all day on writing the conceptual overview for what we're going to need to implement here over the course of time to build flourishing team members who build a flourishing organization. I'm excited and stoked, my friend!" Paul replied.

Jude laughed. "Look at you. Working all day on a Saturday, and you're so excited you can barely contain yourself!"

"You bet," Paul said and laughed along with Jude.

"So, what's next as you develop this 'field manual'? Jude continued. "Is that a fair term to use for what you're working on?"

"That's a great term, Jude! In fact, from now on, that's how we'll refer to it: the Global Solutions Field Manual for building a flourishing organization," Paul replied.

"I like the sound of that, Paul."

"The conceptual framework and definitions are in place; however, I have not yet developed the implementation and the field manual. I was thinking of working from home on Wednesday and knocking that out," Paul said. "Patty will be volunteering at church that day, putting together care packages to hand out at Christmastime, and the kids will be in school all day. I would have the house to myself. What do you think—would you be okay if I did that?"

Jude's eyes widened. "Paul, you do what you think is best. You don't have to ask me for permission for something like that. I trust you." Jude's comment pulled on Paul's heartstrings and tears came to his eyes. "Did I say something I shouldn't have, Paul? What's wrong?" Jude inquired.

"Nothing, boss," Paul answered. "I've longed to hear those words from a boss for decades, but the words never came." He tried to lighten the mood then. "I'm sorry," he said. "I guess I'm getting a little more sentimental and emotional as I get older."

Jude smiled. "Paul, you're my friend and colleague. I trust you completely. I've said it before and will say it again. I couldn't be happier that you're here, and I'm so proud of you. You have exceeded any expectations or hopes that I had when I offered you the job. Keep it up, pal!" Jude gave Paul a quick embrace, and as Paul started to walk away, Jude added, "Let's grab lunch next week after you have Wednesday to do whatever it is you're going to do. Sound like a plan?"

"I can hardly wait, boss…I mean, friend!"

During Monday and Tuesday, Paul was present and engaged, but his mind kept wanting to drift to Wednesday—the day he was going to build out the integration and implementation plan of what he, his team, and his boss had been discussing for weeks. He was so excited at the thought of having the day to build this that he found it more difficult than usual to concentrate. Finally, Wednesday morning came. Paul woke up at 4:00 a.m., wide awake. He didn't even try to go back to sleep because he knew he couldn't. After quietly slipping out of bed, brushing his teeth, and softly walking to the kitchen to make a pot of coffee, Paul sat down at the desk in his study and prepared himself for a full day.

What are the simple, practical steps to integrate empathy into our organization? Paul asked himself as he began typing.

Empathy.

- **Story.** There are few things in life more important and more powerful than "story." Story is so important because each person, as Psalm 139 discusses, is "fearfully and wonderfully made."[20] Each person is unique, and each person has a story that is uniquely theirs. This is normal and each person's story needs to be—must be—told and celebrated. Once someone knows the story of another person, three things happen: (1) others have a greater understanding of the "who" and "why" of the person; (2) others gain a greater appreciation of the person's strengths and limitations (or weaknesses); and (3) a greater compassion occurs, leading to greater grace and mercy. The process and practice for building *empathy* into an organization starts with story, and it looks like this:

[20] Psalm 139 (ESV).

- **Team Story**. Each team—executive, sales, production, maintenance, office, and every other team in the organization—participates. This is an "all-play." Each team schedules time together to share story; whatever it takes and however long it takes. If teams can only schedule an hour at a time over lunch, so be it. When they gather, each person will have the opportunity and the undivided attention of the other team members to share his or her story. This is not the abbreviated summary or bullet-point version; this is the person's full story—from beginning to the present. Ideally, the teams would be able to schedule a block of time long enough for everyone to share their story at the same time; however, that may not be feasible, considering the daily demands on people's time. Regardless, when stories are shared, there must be ample time for everyone to feel like they can share for as long as they desire. If an hour at a time is all that is available for a team of eight people, for example, and it takes thirty minutes per person to share, then it will take four one-hour meetings. They could meet over lunch, or an hour before work, or an hour after work—whatever works best per the schedules and demands of each team. The team leaders will have to work with their teams to find the best way to accomplish this; however, regardless of how, every team member must have the opportunity to share their story.
- **Founder and CEO's Stories.** The founder of the organization's story must be documented. This is critical, historical information that often defines the

"why" of the organization's existence. If possible, the founder's story needs to be recorded—ideally in video and audio format—for everyone in the organization to view, including existing and new team members when they are added. If the current CEO is different from the founder of the organization, the CEO's story also needs to be recorded. It is crucial for the health of the organizational culture that every team member understands the heart, the passion, and the "why" of the highest-ranking leader in the organization. This communicates to everyone that they are part of something bigger than any one person, and it communicates that the organization cares about individuals, not just groups. Knowing the stories of the founder and the senior leader makes them real, personable, and accessible to all team members; it also helps the team members to better understand how what they do contributes to the greater mission of the organization.

Paul finished the section on story and leaned back in his chair. "I love story. It's so powerful," he said. "We need greater emotional intelligence as well. Assessments are great tools for this; however, assessments can be a double-edged sword."

- **Assessments.** Assessments can be a powerful tool for growing in self- and others-awareness, two critical components of emotional intelligence. When used appropriately and healthily, assessments can bring wonderful insight, clarity, and understanding. However, when used inappropriately and unhealthily, assessments can bring damage, destruction, and pain. There are two fundamental keys to using assessments in appropriate and healthy ways: (1) Entrust assessments to trained and certified professionals. They are trained in how to use assessments in the ways they are intended to be used, not presumed to be used. (2) Everyone gets a debrief after an assessment is taken. If a one-on-one debrief is not offered, then that assessment should not be used. It is important to offer both an individual and a team debrief for many reasons, chief of which is learning of new insights at the individual level that may not be revealed if only a team debrief is offered. Some great assessments for both team and individual learning and growth are as follows:

- **DiSC®.** DiSC examines four basic personalities.[21] The key to DiSC is understanding that everyone is a blend of all four personalities, and everyone's blend is unique, which makes every person unique. Most blends are higher in two personalities and lower in two personalities. Some are higher in three and some higher in one, and fewer are considered a "balanced type," which is an even blend of all four personality types. DiSC examines the core motivations of each of the personalities as well as key strengths and weaknesses of each. DiSC is a wonderful assessment tool in team building because it helps team members understand how to communicate more effectively, how to motivate one another, how to leverage strengths, and how to mitigate weaknesses. The power of using the DiSC assessment in organizational culture devel-

[21] https://www.discprofile.com/what-is-disc.

opment comes in helping train team members for greater self-awareness first, and others-awareness second.

- **MBTI®.** Meyers-Briggs Type Indicator (MBTI) has been a go-to assessment for many organizations for decades.[22] MBTI is a preference-based assessment, meaning it helps team members understand both their own as well as their fellow team members' preferences. MBTI examines four dimensions with two characteristics on each dimension. The "energy" dimension examines how a person prefers to recharge their batteries. Some prefer a more "internal" approach by spending time alone or doing solitary activities such as exercising, reading, contemplation, meditation, baking, or other hobbies. Some prefer a more "external" approach by spending time with others or doing activities in groups such as going out to eat or to a bar, going to a concert, playing games, or other group-related activities. The "information" dimension examines how a person prefers to gather the information necessary to make decisions. Some prefer a more "sensing" or "concrete" approach by researching facts, figures, formulas, or completed research studies. Some prefer a more "intuitive" or "gut" approach by trusting one's instincts and past experiences or by making connections from other experiences, knowledge, or concepts. The "decision-making" dimension examines how a person prefers

[22] https://www.myersbriggs.org/my-mbti-personality-type/mbti-basics/.

to make decisions, considering the starting and the stopping point in the decision-making process. Some prefer a more "thinking" or "logical" approach by starting with the facts, the bottom-line, and the conclusions. Some prefer a more "feeling" or "emotional" approach by starting with how one feels about the decision at hand, how the decision will affect other people and relationships, and other emotional issues related to the decision. The key is understanding where one starts in the process and then finishes—because it is nearly always a both-and, not either-or. The final dimension is the "organization" or "flexibility" dimension. Some prefer a more "judgmental" or "regimented" approach to organization, opting for scheduling, to-do lists, advanced planning, elimination of options, and convergence. Some prefer a more "perceiving" or "fluid" approach to organization, including spontaneity, flexibility, spur-of-the-moment, keeping options open, and divergence.

Understanding one's and one's team members' four-letter MBTI combination helps bring clarity, insight, and understanding into the myriad of preferences each person brings with them every day. Understanding these preferences and differences also brings the opportunity to build greater camaraderie as team members understand how preferential differences can bring synergistic results, facilitate more effective communication, and help increase awareness in areas of frustration and misunderstanding.

- **Livstyle.** Livstyle is a multifactor assessment that provides a broad-stroke overview of several assessments.[23] Neatly packaged as a dashboard followed by a detailed report, Livstyle's dashboard examines nine different areas related to personality, preferences, decision-making, motivation, communication, conflict engagement, and team building. When used as a team-building and growing tool, Livstyle is a powerful assessment for growing in self- and others-awareness; it also brings awareness of needed growth, training, and learning as a team.

- **Enneagram.** Enneagram is a tool that has been around for thousands of years. While arguably the best way to engage with Enneagram is through self-study of books, articles, podcasts, and training, there is a credible argument to be made for using Enneagram in a team setting. As with any assessment, having a trained and certified facilitator guide your team is a must; however, when using Enneagram as a team-building exercise, it is even more essential to use an experienced facilitator. One of the easiest-to-use Enneagram assessments is the Wagner Enneagram Personality Style Scales (WEPSS).[24] Built by Jerome "Jerry" Wagner, PhD, the WEPSS Enneagram tool provides great quantitative and qualitative data for self- and others-awareness learning. The report that accompanies the assessment is easy

---

[23] http://findyourlivstyle.com/.

[24] https://www.wepss.com/.

to understand, provides insights and coaching, and provides additional resources for learning. The best way to describe Enneagram is that it is a tool to help people understand their "who," their "what," and their "how." Enneagram dives into the core motivation of each of the nine possible numbers (different types of personalities based on core motivations). As with most assessments, no one is strictly just one number; every person is a combination. With Enneagram, people usually identify with a primary number, a "wing" number, and two other numbers on the diagram that a person accesses in times of stress and health, called accessing the "high side" and the "low side" of these numbers—in other words, displaying the strengths or the weaknesses of these numbers in motivation, behaviors, attitudes, and actions. If Enneagram is chosen as a tool, be fully committed to learning it, working with it, and staying with it for the long term. Because of its depth and its revelatory nature, Enneagram is not an assessment that should be experimented with, used at cursory level, or used once and then not used again. The insights, knowledge, and wisdom that can be gained from Enneagram for self-awareness, others-awareness, and relational learning are phenomenal; however, it takes time—significant time—studying, learning, and discussing to gain the full benefit of the Enneagram.

- **Five Dysfunctions of a Team.** Based upon the book by Patrick Lencioni, *Five Dysfunctions of a Team* is both a powerful book and an assessment for organizations intent on building healthy, engaged, performing teams.[25] The model that Lencioni created starts with the foundation of trust and works up to results.

- **Predictive Index.** Predictive Index is a great tool for helping organizations hire better, build collaborative teams, and motivate engagement.[26] Too often, Predictive Index is used for hiring purposes only; however, when used as part of a more comprehensive team-building approach, the tool is a great facilitator for tracking growth and progress in teams and team members.

As Paul finished typing about assessments, he reflected for a moment. He thought about how the purpose of building empathy in an organization is threefold: (1) build greater emotional intelligence in team members; (2) communicate and listen more effectively together; and (3) demonstrate greater understanding and compassion that comes with knowing one another better. Paul put his hands behind his head and leaned back in his chair. *Why is this important?* he asked himself. *Because one of our core values at Global is that we care about our team members—not just for what they* do *for us but for* who they are *as individuals. Our people are our most important asset, and we must demonstrate that practically. Building flourishing individuals is our focus, and that starts by helping each person grow in self-awareness first, and others-awareness second*, Paul reminded himself. Satisfied with his analysis, he read back over what he

[25] Patrick Lencioni, *The Five Dysfunctions of a Team: A Leadership Fable* (Hoboken: Jossey-Bass, 2002).

[26] https://www.predictiveindex.com/company/.

had just written on the "how to" for building *empathy. If we do these things—share story, invest in assessments for team-member learning and team-building—will this lead to greater empathy?* Paul wondered. *Yes! I believe it will. There are other exercises we could also do, and we can add additional ones over time. However, if we focus on these and do these really, really well, it will make a significant impact on our team members' lives as well as our team unity and performance.*

> **What about you? Which of the *empathy* exercises do you most identify with? What are one, or possibly two, exercises you could implement in your organization, with your team, or personally to intentionally begin to grow in empathy?**

Paul stood up, stretched, and walked to the kitchen to refill his coffee. He yawned as he walked back to his office—feeling a little tired, but excited to keep moving. He sat back down at his desk and prepared to move into the integration and practical implementation of *empowerment.*

Empathy. As Paul stated, there are other activities, practices, and exercises that could be used to grow and build *empathy* in organizations. Story and assessments are two ways; however, there are others to explore. The key is this: doing something is better than doing nothing; do whatever you think, and whatever you feel will be best for your organization at its current stage. Doing something will send the message to your team that you are serious about building flourishing individuals who build flourishing organizations.

Flourishing Life Model as Applied to Organizational Culture. The Flourishing Life Model was included and adapted in this book for four primary reasons:

1. **Tool for growing in self- and others-awareness**. The model is a resource for leaders and managers to have better understanding and insight as to the level they may be at currently, and the levels their team members may also be at currently. Once "here" is known, then a path can be determined for how to get to "there."
2. **Evaluation process input**. Whenever performance is evaluated, during the annual individual development plan (IDP) planning process and during weekly or bi-weekly one-on-one meetings, helping team members both self-evaluate and understand where they currently reside on the Flourishing Life Model is a great opportunity to discuss learning, growth, and development of the team member. Helping team members not only understand but also own their current placement is crucial in helping team members intentionally grow to higher levels in the model.
3. **Leadership development and succession planning**. If leaders desire to build a flourishing organization, then they must be all-in and fully committed to building the desired culture. Knowing which team members are currently at the *flourishing* level—or moving toward it—and knowing which emerging and next-generation potential leaders are also moving toward the *flourishing* level are critical inputs into deciding current and future leadership for the organization.

4. **Accelerators and barriers**. Having each team member read, understand, and then self-evaluate the *accelerators* and the *barriers* that are applicable to them is a beneficial exercise as part of the annual IDP development process. Identifying areas that may be hindering movement, progress, and growth—the *barriers*—can be inputs into growth goals for the year. Identifying areas that may accelerate growth—the *accelerators*—can be inputs to leverage for growth or, possibly, to help overcome identified *barriers*.

As with all the integrational aspects in Part III—the exercises, applications, and examples—there are undoubtedly many other potential uses for the Flourishing Life Model as adapted for organizational culture. The important thing is to understand the model and how it could be utilized within your organization to build flourishing team members who build a flourishing organization.

In the next chapter, we continue our journey with Paul as he outlines the practical exercises for intentionally incorporating *empowerment* into the culture of the organization.

CHAPTER 10

INTEGRATION: EMPOWERMENT

Have you ever been asked to do a task or to help with a project, or been hired to do a job, but then you were not allowed to do what you were asked—or not allowed to do it in the way you knew how? Unfortunately, this happens all too often in organizations where they recruit a team member—often, a highly gifted, experienced, proven leader—who is promised freedom to operate and do what they do in the way they do it best. However, when the team member arrives on the job and the proverbial "honeymoon period" wanes, the rules of the game begin to morph. What may have been overlooked, or where a supervisor may have been silent, now elicits scrutiny or verbal feedback. What may have been allowed now requires permission. What used to be approved quickly and easily now has layers of approvals and bureaucracy. What was once freedom now feels like bondage. What was once blessed is now denied. What was once praised is now criticized.

The point is this: one of the pitfalls of organizational bureaucracy is that they all too often hire gifted, experienced leaders, and then shackle them so they are not able to lead and do what they were hired to do. The other frustration created is hiring gifted, experienced leaders and then not letting them operate as they normally would. Their natural way of operating is criticized or pushed aside, mandating or directing the leader to adopt new ways of operating and leading based on how someone else, often the leader's direct report, operated and led. The priorities of control and conformity overpower shared leadership, creativity, and innovation. Over time, frustration, confusion, and anger arise in the leader's thinking and demeanor, to the point that the leader often resigns or otherwise moves on from the organization. Those who remain are often bewildered at how they either misjudged the leader's contribution potential, or they are at a loss for why the leader they hired was not satisfied and decided to move on. There is always a delicate balance between the necessity of having uniformity and harmony in the team, and individual contribution and creativity. However, this balance can be especially difficult when gifted, experienced leaders are hired into leadership roles. Hiring leaders, but not letting them lead, causes turnover. It is not usually *if* the leader will leave, but *when*.

How do organizations properly empower their team members—especially leaders and managers, those responsible for the growth and development of the team members in organizations? One approach is "command and control," where all power is centralized and concentrated in as few people as possible—usually the CEO, the president, or possibly one or two other executive-level leaders. While this style may work in some organizations, it does not work in organizations where shared leadership and leadership development is of the utmost importance. As organizations grow, shared leadership becomes not just an aspiration; it becomes essential if the organization desires to keep growing and expanding.

For the sake of argument, it is assumed that you, the reader, are not seeking to build a "command and control" organizational culture. As we return to the story of Paul and Global Solutions, we find Paul wrestling with how to build a culture of *empowerment*. The following are exercises and applications that you can also integrate into your organization.

Paul settled back into his chair with a fresh cup of coffee. He stretched his hands and fingers in front of him, and then jumped into the *empowerment* waters. *How do we build a culture of* empowerment *at Global?* Paul pondered. "It starts with having a thorough onboarding process and then having an intentional delegation process," he wrote.

Empowerment.

- **Onboarding.** Onboarding, for some organizations, is viewed as a perfunctory step on a team member's first day. Usually, organizations view it as something to be accomplished as quickly as possible so the team member can "get to work." In organizations focused on building *empowerment* into their cultures, onboarding is one of the most important processes and valuable investments of time into the team member. The onboarding process is the new team member's first experience with the organization post-recruiting. Because onboarding is the process of inculcating team members into the culture of the organization, onboarding begins with the first contact with the then-candidate during the recruiting process. Values are caught more than taught; therefore, the recruiting process must be aligned with the onboarding process, which must be aligned with the values of the organization in turn. The onboarding process must include these elements:

- **Documentation.** It is critically important that the onboarding process be documented with the steps delineated, the rationale for each step, and the team and team member responsible for each step.
- **Communication.** The process must be communicated with every team member—both new and existing.
- **All-Play.** Every team member must go through the onboarding process. If the process is developed after a team member is hired, or if the process is changed, all team members need to work through the process or work through the changes incorporated.

The onboarding process needs to include the following:

- **Hiring Process.** The process must be documented and communicated to a candidate. The hiring process needs to include:
  - **Job description development and posting process.** Each open position must have a job description developed and a process for posting both internally (to provide internal team members an opportunity prior to posting externally) and then externally.
  - **Contact and résumé review.** Candidates express interest and the organization receives and reviews résumés. When the organization proactively pursues candidates, the same process applies.
  - **Introduction.** The hiring liaison or supervisor contacts candidates to meet them and introduce the

organization. If mutual interest is expressed, the candidate is invited into the hiring process.

- **Phone interview.** A formal interview is scheduled. The phone interview should be a time where the candidate shares their story and the interviewer asks several questions to get to know the candidate's values, gifts, conflict-engagement methods, mindset, passion, and motivation.
- **Assessments.** The organization administers its assessments and schedules a debrief with the candidate to discuss the results.
- **Story.** The candidate writes their story and submits it. Alternatively, if this is covered on the phone interview, then sharing one's story with their new team upon hiring could be part of the onboarding process.
- **Interviews.** The candidate is invited to participate in several interviews with team members and leaders in the organization. It is recommended that at least six team members take part in the interviews to provide a diversity of perspectives.
- **Group debrief.** The team members who interview the candidate meet to debrief their interviews. The group debrief could result in a decision to proceed, pause, ask for additional interviews or other information, ask for a spouse interview, or stop the process.
- **Spouse interview.** Usually (but not exclusively) reserved for leadership positions in the organization, the spouse interview is a time for both the candidate

and their spouse to have a more casual interaction with a couple of team members and their spouses. The purpose of this is to allow the candidate's spouse to ask questions and to meet other spouses in the organization.

  - **Offer.** After the hiring process is completed, a written offer is made to the candidate.

- **Onboarding Process.** The onboarding process begins with the acceptance of the written offer.
  - **Gifts sent.** The organization sends a gift box to the candidate and spouse, if applicable. The gift box should include a handwritten note from the team member's direct supervisor, welcoming them to the team, and a shirt or mug (or different swag) with the company's logo. In addition, on the team member's first day, a gift (floral arrangement, food gift box—whatever is gender appropriate) is sent to the spouse.
  - **Day 1.** The team member is greeted at the door by their supervisor when they arrive. The supervisor welcomes them and then introduces them to a member of the human resources team who will be responsible for them for their first day (alternatively, the supervisor may take responsibility for the day). The new team member is taken around and introduced to their new team, trained in the technology of the company, shown the essential areas of the company (restrooms, copy room, exits, break rooms), and introduced to essential teams such as human resources and information technology.

- **First 90, 180, 360 days.** The onboarding process needs to be in ninety-day increments with specific tasks, meetings, and activities assigned during each ninety-day period. Each ninety-day period will vary by department, but every team member's onboarding process needs to include the following:

  - **Culture coach.** Every thirty days, the team member is assigned to a "culture coach." This coach may be from any of the teams in the organization. The coach is responsible to check in weekly for at least one hour with the new team member for relationship building, answering questions, and teaching core constructs and internal lingo (such as acronyms, definitions, and processes).
  - **Books.** Reading the organization's core books is central to culture inculcation and learning of the organization. The list of books is provided during the first week; however, the reading assignments are spread over time, with the core books covered during the team member's first year.
  - **Video and audio training.** Videos welcoming the team member by the CEO, organizational culture training, and other trainings specific to a team member's role are scheduled for review over the course of onboarding.
  - **Rotation.** Over the course of the first year, the new team member will spend time with each team. The amount of time spent with each team will vary. The purpose is twofold: (1) meet as many team members

in the organization as possible, and (2) understand the big picture and how each team contributes to the whole. When it makes sense, team members may also be asked to visit other locations.

- **Constructs, definitions, and lingo.** During the first week, the team member will be given a binder of the core constructs, definitions of terms and acronyms, and other internal lingo and cultural speak that is consistently used or unique to the organization. Over the course of the first ninety days, the team member will be expected to learn these and discuss with their culture coaches.

- **Role training and learning.** The amount of time it takes before the team member begins to function in their role varies based on the role and position within the organization. It is expected that by the end of the first ninety days, the team member is operating in their role; however, proficiency will not be expected until the end of the second ninety days (or whenever is appropriate for the role).

- **IDP:** During the second ninety days, the team member will put together their annual individual development plan. The IDP should contain one to two professional growth goals (with at least one aligned with team goals) and one to two personal growth goals for the ensuing twelve months. The annual IDP should be reviewed with the team member's direct supervisor for their input and feedback. IDP progress should be reviewed quarterly, at a minimum, for accountability and updates on progress toward stated goals.

   - **Quarterly evaluation.** At the end of each quarter, the team member and supervisor meet to do a review of the past quarter. The discussion needs to include what the team member has been learning, areas of excitement as well as frustration, job proficiency growth, organizational culture evaluation, and the focus for the next ninety days.

Paul paused. *Onboarding is a critical piece of building a culture of* empowerment *because it will provide context, insight, and knowledge to each team member; all of these are critical to making wise decisions and acting in the best interest of the organization*, he reflected. *Without these, decision-making will be negatively affected, which will then lead to less empowerment due to questioning of decision-making abilities. Onboarding is the foundational layer for proper* empowerment, Paul concluded before moving on to *delegation.*

- **Delegation.** Empowerment, by definition, means delegated authority to act or decide on behalf of someone else. Shared leadership requires delegated authority. If an *empowerment* culture is desired, delegation must be done very well. Delegation can be trained and taught. The delegation process needs to include the following:
   - **Teaching, Training, and Coaching.** Team members must be fully trained, taught, and coached in their roles.

- **Tools, Resources, and Equipping.** Team members must have the appropriate tools, resources, and equipment necessary to do their jobs fully.
- **Authority.** Delegation means that authority must be given to act and to decide.
- **Responsibility.** Effective delegation means the person being delegated to also has the responsibility for the expected results.
- **Accountability.** Delegation must include accountability. Without accountability, the temptation when things do not go as planned or expected is for the person's supervisor to step in and take over the situation until it is fixed or corrected. The key to accountability is holding someone accountable for results. When the results are not realized or expectations are not met, the key is to *not* focus on the results to fix the problem. Focusing on getting better results often causes an individual to work longer or harder but does not address the root cause. The focus needs to be on the *inputs* and *activities*, *NOT* the results. With unsatisfactory results, focusing on the inputs and activities used in producing the results provides the opportunity to address the root cause(s) of the problem.
- **Evaluation.** If results are repeatedly not realized, the evaluation needs to include the following:
  - **Tools, skills, knowledge.** If the team member lacks these, it is the responsibility of the organization to provide these to the team member.

- **Attitude, desire, experience.** If the team member lacks these, it is incumbent upon the team member to either change, get counseling or coaching, get experience—inside or outside the organization—or pursue a different role.

- **Leadership in Delegation.** Delegation needs to be an intentional process that ensures proper equipping, training, handing off responsibility, and holding accountable. Consider this proven process as you delegate:
  - "I do. You watch." Start by communicating your intentions of empowering someone else to do something you are currently doing. Don't just hand it off and say, "There you go. Best of luck!" That is not effective delegation. Bring the team member alongside and show them what you do, how you do it, and why you do it.
  - "We do together." After the team member learns what you are doing, do it together—side by side.
  - "You do. I coach." After doing it together and gaining confidence, allow the team member to do it while you observe and coach. The goal is not that the team member does it exactly like you do; the goal is effectiveness and results. The team member may have or find a more effective way to do it than you, which is great. Celebrate that!
  - "You do. We celebrate." Celebrate when the team member has fully owned what you delegated and is doing it effectively.

- "We do. We train others." Now that two team members can effectively do what was delegated—you and the team member you delegated to—there are now two people who can train and delegate to others when needed. This is now moving from addition to multiplication.

As Paul finished the section on delegation, he went back through what he had written. *Is this enough to build a culture of empowerment?* he wondered. *The key will be in how we both train and execute these. The key will always be in execution.* "We can have the best plans and intentions, but if we do not follow through, live what we say we believe, and execute with excellence, these are all just hollow and meaningless platitudes without substance," Paul said aloud.

> **What about you? Which of the *Empowerment* exercises did you most identify with? What are one, or possibly two, exercises that you could implement in your organization, with your team, or with you personally to intentionally begin to grow in empowerment?**

Empowerment. *Empowerment* in organizations can be difficult, but it is necessary, especially as organizations grow. When an organization is just starting or it is a small team, it is easier—sometimes necessary—to have centralized decision-making. In the start-up phase in organizations, it is necessary for the founder's voice to be the dominant voice and the founder's decisions to be primary. As organizations grow and expand—especially geographically, but in revenue and number of team members as well—it becomes increasingly crucial to move to a shared, delegated leadership style of governance. Organizations that keep decisions centralized and controlled by one or a few will limit their growth potential, or they will have difficulty retaining gifted, experienced leaders because they will feel shackled and stifled in their ability to lead.

Developing robust hiring and onboarding processes and being intentional about how delegation is trained and executed will help in building a culture of empowerment. These are not the only processes or ways to build a culture of empowerment; other processes, practices, and exercises could also be incorporated. The key to building healthy, flourishing organizational culture where team members flourish is to be intentional about it. If leadership does nothing to intentionally develop culture, it will develop on its own. Organizational culture is a given in every organization; it happens whenever two or more people are present. So why not build the kind of culture that you desire? It won't happen by accident or by not investing in it. The examples, practices, and processes I gave in Part III are examples of proven methodologies and practices you can incorporate into your organization to intentionally build your desired culture.

In the next chapter, Paul dives into *excellence*, the third and final piece of the "un-formula" formula for building flourishing organizations.

CHAPTER 11

INTEGRATION: EXCELLENCE

Have you ever been part of a championship-caliber team—maybe a team that won a conference championship, regional championship, or state championship? Or, have you been part of a team such as an orchestra or a choir or ensemble, and you couldn't wait until the next practice or performance because the music produced together was utterly amazing? Maybe you have been part of a project team or task force that was assigned an especially challenging problem to solve. Did you not only solve the problem, but did it ahead of schedule, under budget, and with creativity and innovation that impressed everyone—even the big boss?

Excellence is contagious. When a team is excellent, it produces excitement and attracts others to it. When a team is underperforming, or doesn't care if they win or lose, or when mediocre is acceptable, it is difficult to stay motivated or be excited. Unfortunately, many organizations and many teams within organizations reach a point where the status quo becomes acceptable. Mediocrity becomes tolerated, and playing offense switches to playing—and staying on—defense. Doing what is necessary to get by becomes the predominant mindset. When this begins to creep into organizational culture, motivation and excitement quickly give way to complacency and boredom. Where a commitment to *excellence* may have once been the organizational norm, a commitment to *good enough* becomes the new norm. What do organizations do to ensure that a commitment to *excellence* stands the test of time along with changes or succession in leadership? As with anything related to organizational culture, it requires intentionality, consistent and frequent communication, and documenting processes and procedures to memorialize the core practices and methodologies of the organization. To see what this looks like in practice, let's return once again to Paul's journey at Global Solutions.

After Paul finished his lunch, he returned to his study; he knew he was getting close to the finish line, and he was excited and a little anxious at the same time. He was excited because he couldn't wait to move from planning and documenting to implementing as he trained his team. Working as a team, they would then train the entire organization. He was anxious because he knew the importance of what they were doing—breaking ground and laying the foundation for years, perhaps decades, to come. While it didn't have to be perfect, it needed to be simple to understand, practical, and implementable, and it had to produce the intended results.

Paul returned to his computer and began to type as he started the section on *excellence*. "Excellence is a word often used to evaluate the quality of a task, product, service, or result. How do we build a *culture of excellence* at Global Solutions? The key is to build a culture and mindset where *excellence* isn't the exception. *Excellence* is expected; it is the norm, and part of the standard operating procedures of everything we do at Global. In addition, we must make sure we are both listening to and communicating with our team members. *Excellence* is what we do and who we are; it is our legacy," Paul concluded.

Excellence.

- **Processes and Procedures.** To build a culture of *excellence,* organizations must pursue, implement, and document best practices. When a more effective way of doing something is discovered that makes the organization more excellent, processes and procedures must be updated. Processes and procedures cannot be so fixed or unchangeable that when a more effective way is found, the current ways of doing things cannot be updated.
    - **Documentation.** The documenting of processes and procedures starts by identifying those team members who are proficient and produce excellent results consistently. It is critical to document the "what," "why," and "how" of their role, their mindset, and their practices so the organization can train others in the organization as well as their successors when the time comes.
    - **Succession Planning.** The more removed from the founder the organization becomes, the greater the risk for mission drift—as discussed earlier—and the greater the risk for tolerance of behaviors, attitudes, and practices that would not have been accepted at one time. One of the benefits of documenting the values of the organization as well as best practices is succession planning. When a team member leaves an organization, replacing someone for a role is one thing; replacing someone for a role with the same

dedication to excellence is another. Documenting best practices helps accelerate the learning curve for new team members during the onboarding process of learning the role.

- **Ownership Mentality.** Paul recalled a time he and Patty had eaten at a nice restaurant before they moved to Nashville. Paul was so impressed with the servers at this restaurant because even though each table had its own server, multiple other servers waited on their table throughout the evening, refilling water, removing dirty dishes, and bringing food. Paul asked their server, "Why does it seem that the servers here help with other tables and are not protective of their own tables?" The server had a big grin come over her face. "Ah, well that is simple," she replied. "Here, every table is my table!" As Paul recalled that conversation from over a year ago, he exclaimed, "That's it! That is the mindset we must teach, train, and reward at Global. Team members must internalize the concept: *every team, every project, every customer, every task is my team, my project, my customer, and my task!*" An owner cares about every part and every detail of the organization. As the organization grows, however, it eventually reaches a point where the owner can no longer know every detail of the organization, which is why choosing leaders with whom to share leadership—and then teaching, training, coaching, and rewarding them for what is vitally important—is so crucial in organizational development and growth. Bestowing an "owner's mentality" throughout the organization from top to bottom—not just the top—may seem like trying to climb the world's highest mountain, but it can be done; it must be done. As with most things, there is rarely a shortcut or magic formula. Bestowing an owner's mentality of unwavering excellence throughout the organization means doing three things with excellence:

- **Onboarding.** The process of bestowing an owner's mentality starts on day one—actually, it starts with the first contact when the team member is in the recruiting process. But the process of building an owner's mentality begins in earnest on the team member's first day. Every teaching, every training, every coaching moment, every meeting, every opportunity must be laser-focused on ingraining the concept and the principle of adopting an owner's mentality and mindset. If a piece of trash is on the floor and you didn't throw it there, pick it up; if the sidewalk needs to be shoveled in the wintertime and the person who normally does that is plowing the parking lot, shovel the walkway. If the restroom is out of toilet paper, restock it; if the microwave in the break room looks like someone blew something up in it, clean it. If a fellow colleague is overwhelmed with something, offer to help; if an item was missed for a customer order, offer to deliver it or ship it to them. And the list goes on. The bottom line is this: if adopting an owner's mentality is important, then silos, territorialism, withholding information, possessiveness, defensiveness, attacking, and other bad behaviors have no place in the organization and must not be tolerated; this mentality starts on day one.

- **Hire slowly. Fire quickly.** Too often, organizations get this backwards. When positions need to be filled and the feeling of desperation to fill those positions sets in, the temptation becomes increasingly great to hire the first person who seems like they could do the job. While this may wind up working out, there is a high risk it will not, and then the organization is in a quandary of figuring out how to address the problem. On the other end of the team-member life cycle, organizations are often reluctant to fire quickly—even when it is painfully obvious to all (including the team member) that the job isn't working out as anyone had hoped. Proper processes and steps should be followed to provide the team member the opportunity to address performance issues or even move to a different role, especially if the issue is a lack of skill or experience; however, when processes are followed and opportunities are given and it still isn't working out, it is time to have the difficult conversation and allow the team member to succeed elsewhere. It is very difficult to release a team member who is well-liked but struggles with performance; however, when there is a character issue, an attitude problem, or a lack of desire, then organizations must act more swiftly in either correcting the offending behavior or removing the team member. Allowing flawed character, bad attitudes, or lack of desire to remain in the organization is the equivalent of condoning, and when left unaddressed, these undesired attitudes and behaviors begin to spread like wildfire throughout the organization. Allowing one bad apple will eventually lead others to rot, and before the organization knows what happened, a root of toxicity takes hold within the culture of the organization.

- **Aligned reward systems.** Building an owner's mentality of unwavering commitment to excellence throughout the organization will not happen by accident; it requires intentionality, repeated communication, and rewarding desired attitudes and behaviors. Organizational reward systems—commissions, bonuses, incentives, performance awards—are usually tied to results, as they should be. Organizations that are intent and focused on building healthy, engaged, flourishing cultures should put reward and incentive systems into place that recognize, praise, and reward the attitudes and behaviors that are consistent and aligned to the core values the organization desires.

As Paul put down the final period on processes and procedures, he paused for a moment before moving on to one-on-one meetings. *We need to review the processes and procedures across the organization*, Paul thought to himself. *If we are serious about building a culture where our team members adopt an owner's mentality of unwavering commitment to excellence, we must have the support systems in place from top to bottom that communicate this consistently."*

- **One-on-ones.** "Over time, our team members will forget, get distracted, become tired, and grow weary; we all do," Paul wrote. "Our leaders must have regular contact with every other team member in our organization. It may not be feasible to have a weekly meeting, but no more than two weeks should go by without a face-to-face between leaders and supervisors and the team members they lead," he continued. Many organizations encourage—even require—supervisors and their direct reports to have regular one-on-one meetings; however, too often, these one-on-ones are not productive, and they often become a dreaded meeting on team members' calendars. Effective one-on-one meetings are not a time for performance evaluations, lectures, or one-sided communication; too often, this is how they are treated. Effective one-on-ones should include the following:

  - **Manageable Number.** Supervisors who have too many direct reports often have difficulty effectively leading because they are caught up in the tyranny of the urgent, solving daily problems, or responding to critical issues. The ideal number of direct reports should be four to six for senior leadership and middle management. Front-line management and supervisors may be able to have ten to fifteen direct reports; however, when the number of direct reports exceeds ten for *any* supervisor, it becomes increasingly difficult for the supervisors to invest time, energy, and resources into their direct reports. There is an inverse correlation between the number of direct reports and the excitement and joy a supervisor experiences.

Once the number of direct reports exceeds five to six for senior and middle management or exceeds ten for front-line management, leader satisfaction decreases.

- **Scheduled Time.** While the occasional spontaneous one-on-one is acceptable, one-on-ones need to be scheduled—ideally on the same day, at the same time, and for the same length of time. Ideally, supervisors and their team members would meet one-on-one weekly; however, with larger teams, weekly meetings may not be feasible. With larger teams, a biweekly meeting would be acceptable; however, going longer than every other week without a face-to-face is too long.
- **One Hour.** Having one-on-ones is meant to be short, sweet, and to the point. If a longer discussion is necessary to address performance issues, or if there is another matter that the team member needs to discuss that will take longer than an hour, another time should be scheduled. The goal is to make one-on-ones predictable, enjoyable, and positively anticipated; however, when one-on-ones consistently run longer than the scheduled time or conversations occur that should not occur in that meeting, then one-on-ones become dreaded and lose their function and purpose.
- **Shared Time.** The one-hour time is shared between the supervisor and the team member. The first thirty minutes belong to the team member; whatever the team member wants to discuss, that time belongs to them. The second thirty minutes belong to the

supervisor; whatever the supervisor wants to discuss, that time is theirs. For clarity, the two thirty-minute time periods are not intended to be thirty-minute monologues. The time is intended to be a dialogue; however, the topics of discussion are determined by the team member for the first thirty minutes and the supervisor for the second thirty minutes.

- **Positive and Memorable.** One-on-ones should be a positive and memorable experience for both the supervisor and their direct reports. The time should be positively anticipated on both sides. The purpose of one-on-ones is to communicate that every team member is seen, heard, and valued; every team member has a place in the organization, and what they do contributes value. The one hour of time invested weekly or biweekly is a time to build relationships, share (or reshare) vision, appreciate the "what," and more importantly, appreciate the "who."

As Paul finished, a wave of emotion came over him from seemingly out of nowhere. "What is that?" Paul asked himself as he wiped his eyes. *What we are trying to build here at Global Solutions is so important*, he pondered then. *This will influence, impact, and change people's lives—inside the organization from top to bottom, and outside of the organization as our team members interact with their families, customers, vendors, and the community. Building flourishing team members who build a flourishing organization…I would have never thought I would get to be part of something like this. I am so excited, humbled, and even scared, if I am being completely honest. The importance of building this and doing this well is exciting but is also a burden.*

Paul acknowledged that it would take time, energy, and resources to build; it would take an all-in, day-in-and-day-out commitment. It would not be one-and-done; it would be in-the-trenches, daily-grind stuff. The keys would be to communicate, practice, communicate, live it, communicate, improve, communicate, and communicate some more. *This will be difficult and there will be disappointment and frustration along the way*, Paul thought. *However, the impact it will have on our team members' lives, their families, and the communities in which we work, live, play, and worship will make this worth everything we do.* And with that, Paul wiped his eyes, saved his work, and powered down his computer. The easy part—planning and documenting—was finished; the hard part—implementing, teaching, and training—was about to begin. Paul couldn't wait for his lunch with Jude the following week. He planned to have everything formatted into a "field manual" format and be ready to discuss it with Jude at lunch. Based upon the conversations he had already had with Jude, he anticipated full support, full engagement, and being all-in. Paul was ready to go!

> **What about you? Which of the *excellence* exercises did you most identify with? What are one, or possibly two, exercises you could implement in your organization, with your team, or with you personally to intentionally begin to grow in excellence?**

Excellence. Building a mindset of unwavering commitment to excellence is not something that is taught once and then never discussed again; it takes repeated communication, reminding, and coaching to take incremental steps of continually improving to become more excellent. As in other parts, the examples provided here are not an exhaustive list; the important thing is to put into place whatever works for your organization to take the steps necessary toward building a culture of unwavering commitment to excellence.

Our journey has now brought us to our final chapter. I will conclude by pulling out the map and reviewing where we have been together, and then we will say our farewell with a call to action, so you will have definitive next steps as you continue your own journey, picking up where ours ends.

CLOSING

ENGAGED AND FLOURISHING

As promised, here is the rest of the football story I began in the Introduction:

In 2016, a small high school in Butler, Indiana, hired a football coach for its struggling varsity football team. Coach Todd Mason was an alumnus of Eastside High School who had one overarching focus: to one day return to his alma mater and finish unfinished business: winning the state championship.

When the coach arrived, he implemented a vision statement: "All In," and a mission statement: "Do Right." Four words that, over the course of the next seven years, would transform not just a football team but also the individual players, the families, the coaching staff, the school, and the community. The vision and mission were the focus. Period.

Coach patiently waited for years. He planned and executed with methodical precision and excellence. One of the first things Coach did was implement a new system of discipline. Affectionately naming the program "Speed School," Coach required the players coming out of eighth grade to be at the school at 6:00 a.m. three days a week, every week. The players gained speed, strength, and coordination. They also began to bond as a team.

In addition to Speed School, Coach also began enforcing consequences for behaviors that were inconsistent with All In and Do Right. During the first couple of seasons, many players faced the consequences of their negative behaviors and attitudes, with many missing more than one game due to suspensions. Coach endured many phone calls from upset parents during the first two seasons asking why players were suspended or their playing time reduced. He used these calls as opportunities to share his vision and mission. The parents began to understand what All In and Do Right meant. By year three, the number and frequency of phone calls subsided dramatically, and years four through seven yielded a whopping one phone call…total. By year six, an entire community was benefiting from four words that became not just a focus for a team but also a rallying cry for a community.

Coach consistently demonstrated the key fundamentals and principles of building an engaged team. He demonstrated genuine *empathy* by caring deeply and personally for these players and their families. He provided the tools, the training, the coaching, and the preparation necessary so that when the time came for these young players to take the field as varsity players, they would be fully *empowered* and capable of doing what they had worked so hard to do. He maintained an unwavering commitment to *excellence* in everything from planning and preparation to training, conditioning, team-building, and mental toughness.

After years of preparation and planning, this team's time had come; they were ready. During Coach's final four years, the team won their conference all four years, won their sectional championship three of four years, won their regional championship once, and in a heart-breaking loss in their semi-state championship, their dreams of making it to the state championship game fell short by just three points.

The following year, the players, parents, staff, and even coaches wondered both privately and publicly what kind of a season would unfold next. Not wavering from the discipline nor his original plan, the coach kept the team focused and engaged on doing what they had been trained to do. The team went on to win the next eight games in a row, falling in the sectional championship game after being in the lead, but losing the star quarterback early in the second quarter.

The young men who played as Eastside Blazer football players between 2016 and 2022 were part of a special experience. The lessons bestowed on these players, coaches, families, and a community were both life-changing and life-giving. Even though Coach did not bring home the desired state championship trophy, everyone directly or indirectly involved was changed and impacted. Character is built by training, hard work, and practice. Character is revealed on the field of play, and every single person is on some field every day. Whether your field is a football field, a professional office, a boardroom, or a dining room, the bottom line is the same: character is built and revealed in day-to-day life. Coach and his staff not only knew this but also lived it. He built a legacy of excellence year after year by teaching consistency, working hard, being intentional, and not wavering from the vision and mission.

Coach Mason understood that culture is paramount in building a winning team and in building something bigger than himself. As we have explored through our journey, building a healthy, flourishing culture requires intentionality, hard work, and perseverance. Not everyone is going to get the what or the why when changes are introduced to "the way we have always done things." In addition, there may be some who openly go against what you are trying to build; however, let me encourage you to keep pressing on, stay the course, and finish the race. Very few would say that going through the process of changing a culture is an easy or fast process; however, nearly everyone would say that it was worth it. Remember what this is all about: people. People are worth it. The stakes are too high to not do this. Considering the number of hours adults spend working, it is both an opportunity and a responsibility for organizations to intentionally build the healthiest culture possible so their team members can flourish. Doing anything less seems equivalent to malpractice.

Can you imagine what it was like being part of a team like Coach Mason's—a team that struggled mightily its first three years, and then experienced unparalleled success for the next four? Was it easy? No! It took hard work, hours of preparation, and unwavering dedication to intentionally build a team and a culture like this. It is the same with any team or organization. What does the thought of working in or building a flourishing organization—like being part of a winning team like Coach Mason's—do for you? Does it bring excitement? Does it bring anxiety? Perhaps after the journey we have had together, you are not convinced this is even possible. Or maybe you are asking why organizations would even want to do this. Why would organizations want to commit the time, energy, and resources necessary to build flourishing team members who build flourishing organizations? The reality is that not every organization will want to do whatever it takes to build a flourishing culture—and that is okay—but some organizations will. This field manual is for those who want to build a flourishing organization.

What about you? If you like the idea of working in or building a flourishing organization, what is one thing you could put into practice in your leadership to influence your organization?

To review our journey of what it takes, let's pull out our map and evaluate our journey from there to here. What does the big-picture map reveal to us? Engaged and flourishing team members who are building engaged and flourishing organizations. The overview looks likc this:

- **The "Un-Formula" Formula.** We started our journey by examining what engaged and excited teams are and how organizations can intentionally build them. Using the phrase the "un-formula" formula, we started by defining engaged teams and then looked at three core functions of building engaged and excited teams.
    - **Engaged Teams.** Engaged teams means having team members who are excited to come to work and are engaged when they are there. Engaged teams are intentionally built by demonstrating empathy, delegating empowerment, and having an unwavering commitment to excellence.
    - **Empathy.** Demonstrating empathy involves communicating that team members are seen, heard, and cared for—not only for *what they do* but also for *who they are.* Listening, story, and assessments help team members grow in self- and others-awareness, which are key ingredients to emotional intelligence.
    - **Empowerment.** Empowerment means delegating authority and responsibility, with accountability, to act and decide on matters related to one's role.
    - **Excellence.** Bestowing an unwavering commitment to excellence in organizations means building the

support systems necessary to intentionally communicate and reward the importance of having an owner's mentality, continual improvement, and accepting nothing less than excellence from every team member.

- **Flourishing Life Model Applied to Building Flourishing Organizations.** Building on the Flourishing Life Model as presented in *unSatisfied: When Less Is More,* we journeyed through the model, applying it to team members in the organization. The purpose of this model was to have a tool to evaluate where each team member currently resides on the model, and to have a road map for each team member to move to flourishing, if that is what they desire to do.
    - **Diminishing.** Has all but given up or wants to quit.
    - **Surviving.** Does whatever it takes to get through the day.
    - **Striving.** Intentionally learns and grows to improve position, takes on a new role, or gains new skills and knowledge.
    - **Thriving.** Performs consistently at a high level; consistently contributes great value to organization; often a leader.
    - **Flourishing.** Focused on investing and developing team members, legacy, team over self, and being part of something bigger than self.

If building a flourishing organization is the stated desire of the leadership of the organization, then it is crucial that the leaders of the organization are all-in and fully committed to building flourishing team members. Having team members in leadership positions who are not committed to pursuing living at the *flourishing* level would be contrary to the stated values and desires of the organization. Being committed to building a flourishing organization requires leaders who are pursuing living at the *flourishing* level. As with anything, perfection is not the goal. Commitment to *flourishing*, intentional living, and the pursuit thereof are the goals.

- **Integration and Implementation.** It is important that leaders help foster an environment of intentional energy and effort. Integration and implementation require full investment in doing whatever it takes to build necessary processes, procedures, and practices to build flourishing team members who build a flourishing organization.
    - **Empathy.** Incorporate story and assessments into the fabric of your organizational culture. The purpose is not to pry, label, or pigeonhole; the purpose is to understand, to know, and to be known. Reflect upon the last time you heard someone share their story for the first time; perhaps it was someone you had known for quite some time, but you had never heard their story. What was your perspective of them prior to knowing their story? After? Story makes a huge difference in relationships and in organizations. Assessments, when administrated and debriefed by a trained facilitator, lead to insights, understanding, and connections that create bonds and relational glue that leads to greater relational effectiveness. The bottom line is this: if you want to build or increase

empathy in your organization, start sharing story and assessments.

- **Empowerment.** Developing and implementing a robust onboarding process and procedure lays a solid foundation for communicating the importance of investing in training and culture to provide the opportunity for every team member's long-term success with the organization. Learning to delegate effectively communicates the importance of shared leadership, responsibility, authority, and accountability. Knowing that shared leadership is important sends the message that empowerment is not just giving lip service; rather, it is a value the organization practices.
- **Excellence.** Excellence is a practice that starts with a mindset. Establishing a corporate culture where excellence is expected—and nothing less than excellence is accepted—is critical if the organization desires to be excellent and produce excellence. Having processes and procedures in place that align the organizational values to the evaluation and reward systems is crucial. Communicating repeatedly the "what," "how," and "why" is vital to keep the organization aligned to its core intent and values. Expecting that every team member adopts an ownership mentality is important to steward the resources and produce excellent results from top to bottom. Having meaningful and effective conversations—especially one-on-ones—are critical to fostering a culture of continuous improvement, learning, and growth, which are all vital to fostering excellence in organizations.

As a reminder, the examples and practices provided are not exhaustive lists. There are other examples and practices that would serve as catalysts in building flourishing organizations built upon the pillars of empathy, empowerment, and excellence. The important thing is not that every possible example or practice is delineated; the important thing is to pick *something* and start. The key is not in knowing the concepts; the key is in the execution. Start today and start somewhere to begin building a flourishing organization.

If you would like to know more about these examples and practices or if you would like to explore ways in which I could assist you or your organization, please do not hesitate to contact me. My contact information is in the About the Author section.

FINAL CALL TO ACTION

As our journey together comes to an end, your journey—I hope—is just beginning. The journal of notes you kept with you on our journey together is full of wonderful thoughts, ideas, dreams, and hopes for you and for your organization. Use this journal as a reminder of your journey along with this book, a "field manual" in its own right, to make a difference where you are planted in your organization. Whether you own, lead, or work in an organization, the decision to move forward in building flourishing individuals who build flourishing organizations is up to you.

- If you *own* the organization, start today by picking one area to implement one practice. Start with story, for example. Pull your team together and spend time sharing one another's story with each other. The key isn't *where* you start; the key is *that* you start. Pick something and start as soon as possible.
- If you are *one of the leaders* in the organization, leverage your leadership position to bring positive change. If getting widespread adoption is not possible at first, start with the team you lead. Incorporate one of the

practices with your team, make note of the differences that are made within your team members and the way your team works together, and then share with the other leaders what is happening on your team. The key isn't to change the entire organization all at once; the key is to change what you are able to change and influence others to bring change as well.

- If you are *a team member* in the organization, share with your other team members and your leader or supervisor. Share the concepts that capture your imagination and ask if there is one thing that you could do with your team. If people aren't receptive at first, then ask your other team members if they would like to meet outside of work to share stories together as a potential starting point. The key isn't to influence your supervisor to adopt everything and go all-in at once; the key is to influence your supervisor to try something, and nothing speaks louder than changed behaviors, attitudes, and actions. As you and your team members change and improve, it will get the attention of your supervisor. When your supervisor asks what is making the difference, you will have an opportunity to use your voice.

And that brings us to the end of our journey together. As with any journey, the most important step is the first step; making the decision to move and do something is often the most difficult part of any new adventure. Please know you are not alone. There are many leaders and many organizations who are on this journey. It is not easy—it is difficult. There are potholes, road closures, detours, and barriers to navigate, and there will be setbacks and disappointments; however, the key is to stay committed to the journey, fully knowing that the path from here to there is never a straight line.

Are you ready to start your journey where ours concludes? I hope and pray that you are. Leadership is a wonderful responsibility and a tremendous burden. It is a wonderful responsibility because every day, you have the opportunity to have a positive influence for good in the lives around you. It is a tremendous burden because life is all about people, and as leaders, people look up to and evaluate leaders' attitudes, behaviors, thinking, reactions, and communication. Life is wild, short, and precious. You only have one journey through the living of this life.

There are two ways to live this life. The first way of living is doing whatever you want, when you want, with no regard for others—their well-being, their growth, their needs, their preferences. More than likely, this way of living will lead to regrets, disappointments, and disillusionment. Placing your own comfort above everything and everyone else, while fun and beneficial for a season, leads to a life of loneliness, emptiness, and hollowness. The second way of living is living for something greater than oneself with a focus on relationships—with God and others. Know that life is bigger than you. Everyone is created with a "God-shaped hole" in their souls that can only be filled and satisfied by a relationship with God. Without that relationship, you and I would spend our lives trying to find satisfaction, meaning, and purpose by filling it with the pursuit of money, power, possessions, sex, activities, hobbies, accomplishments, work, volunteering, success, tasks, food, or whatever else that seems appealing to fill the hole in our soul that only a relationship with God can fill. There are greater purposes and callings we have in life: investing in others, seeing others' needs, and doing whatever we can do to help instead of ignoring the needs; knowing others' preferences and deferring to those preferences, at times, instead of fighting against them; and accepting that life is intended to be lived with others in relationship together, not alone or climbing over others to get ahead. And living life "from now to then," focusing on what you want to be remembered for at the end of your life by aligning your "who," "what," and "why" to your desired values and priorities—so that when you reach the end of your life's journey, your story looks how you hoped it would. For me, that means arriving at the end of my journey and hearing God say, "Well done, good and faithful servant." I pray the same for you.

Life is difficult and life is very good at throwing curve balls—sometimes daily. The only constant in life is change. If this is true, then make the choice to live life intentionally wherever you work, live, play, and worship. Make the choice to pursue a flourishing life and influence others to do the same. And if you own, lead, or work in an organization, make the decision today to take one step to influence your organization to build flourishing team members who build flourishing organizations. May it be so!

EPILOGUE

You may be curious about what happened to Paul's previous employer, Strategic Concepts, Inc. The bottom line is this: Paul's instincts were spot on, and he left just in time. Originally, the culture of the organization was healthy and flourishing. People genuinely cared for one another, the team accomplished good work, and good results were often followed by even better results. But then it began to change to an unhealthy, toxic culture without trust, without empathy, without empowerment, and without excellence. Shortly after Paul left, Strategic hired a new CEO. As is too often the case, the new CEO quickly replaced many of the C-suite positions, filling them with his "buddies" when they were not the best qualified people for the jobs. When the new CEO arrived along with his corresponding larger-than-life ego and self-centered focus, the culture accelerated its previously slow downhill slide and quickly fell off of the proverbial cliff.

The new CEO could, unfortunately, truly be categorized as a narcissist. What used to be strategic leadership meetings focusing on vision, growth, and planning for the organization soon became meetings focused on how to build the

CEO's personal image, brand, and platform. Collaborative and cross-functional teams working together on both strategic and tactical projects quickly turned into protective silos where teams fought one another. The little remaining trust completely eroded. Blame-shifting, taking credit for others' work, public confrontation, and deriding team members to elevate others became the day-to-day norm.

While the internal mechanisms of the company became more toxic, in disarray, and chaotic, to the external world there were subtle but noticeable changes. Response times to clients and potential clients changed from near-immediate to a day, or even days. Timelines for work product that were once promised and strictly adhered to were now unexplainably changed, with Strategic committing to few or no new timelines for both existing and new client work. Errors, which were previously few and very far between, were now frequent and common. Where the marketing campaigns once aimed at building the brand and platform of Strategic Concepts, Inc., now they focused on building the personal brand and platform of the CEO. The CEO's new branding successfully elevated him over the company from a branding perspective, but that was not the only way he elevated himself, as the entire company learned in less than two years under his leadership.

Even though the culture of Strategic Concepts continued to decline and become increasingly toxic, some of the original team members stayed. The remaining team bought into and were committed to the original vision, mission, and purpose of the company. They expressed their concerns to the new leadership team. A handful of faithful team members, for example, scheduled a two-hour meeting with the new CEO and his new team. They meticulously outlined what they loved about Strategic Concepts, the principles and practices that had made the company so special. Even though the concepts and terms were not familiar to the new CEO and his new team, the original team members cogently described the kind of culture that had once existed: a culture of empathy—genuine care and concern for team members and treating everyone as valued humans; empowerment—the sharing of authority and responsibility, with accountability, to make decisions and get results; and excellence—an unwavering commitment to excellence in processes, procedures, and outcomes.

After the original team members' impassioned presentation, the new leadership team seemed to demonstrate genuine care and concern, saying that transition and change are difficult, but things would soon be better than ever! However, instead of seeing improvements and positive change, the culture continued its downward slide. The original team members did what they could to try to influence change and preserve the original culture, but they were soon overwhelmed and overrun, and they also quickly realized that the new leadership team was very gifted at gaslighting and corporate politics. Occasionally, one of the original, committed team members would resign or be dismissed, often for unknown reasons, but there was never a mass exodus. Despite the internal mess, somehow the company continued to grow in revenue and produce results for its customers and clients; however, what none of the 100+ team members realized was how the company's finances were being handled behind the corporate veil of senior leadership.

Then, the dreaded day came. Without warning, the company's leadership announced they were done. Completely finished. Out of money and out of business. Even though the announcement was sudden and took most of the team members by surprise, there had actually been several breadcrumbs dropped along the path to insolvency. Strategic Concepts had made payments that came back with insufficient funds, payroll was missed, vendors started putting the company on COD (cash on delivery) rather than extending credit, and credit collection agencies began calling and sending letters. The growing debt issues were unknown to most of the team members; however, when Strategic missed payroll, it sent a huge ripple through the organization. Leadership tried to shift the blame to the payroll processing company, but it soon became known that the payroll was missed because the company had no money.

In one fell swoop, all but a handful of team members—many of them loyal and dedicated team members with years of service—were out of a job. Some were outright fired. Most were laid off. Strategic and the CEO said it was temporary, but that was another slick scheme of leadership trying to protect what little image and reputation remained. The handful of remaining team members were given strict instructions and threatened with immediate termination if they deviated from communicating the company tale that this was all temporary as part of a corporate restructuring. Soon, the company promised, everyone would be rehired, the company's clients would be serviced, they would fully honor their contracts, and the company would be stronger than ever! Gifted writers in public relations wrote new lies to gaslight and mislead the public to avoid a mass exodus of Strategic Solutions' remaining clients, and to keep creditors from filing lawsuits.

Time went on and more of the internal workings of the company were made known. Allegations of misappropriation and comingling of funds emerged. Even stronger allegations were leveled such as defrauding, intentionally misleading, and embezzlement. As days turned into weeks, and then months, it became painfully obvious to all that a corporate restructuring was indeed not in the works, or if it was, then there was just too big of a mess to be able to restructure and reemerge. Those team members who had initially taken a wait-and-see approach began to polish up their resumes and search for jobs. Others decided to hang out a shingle and try business on their own. And then the lawsuits began: first the creditors, then the clients for nonperformance on contracts—especially those who had prepaid but received no service. It was obvious to all that this once thriving, successful company with a rock-solid reputation around the world had crumbled—leaving a trail of devastation both inside and outside the organization. Lives were broken. Relationships were torn. And bewilderment, anger, and even fury reigned for a moment in many of the hearts and minds of the wonderful people affected by the incompetence, malfeasance, and narcissism of this now ex-CEO.

Unfortunately for Paul, he was not completely immune to what was happening. Paul had invested nearly two decades of his life at Strategic Solutions. He had many colleagues who were still his friends, and with whom he maintained some level of contact over the years. At first, it was an email here or there from his friends expressing their frustration and bewilderment. Then, the texts and phone calls came—most of them emotionally charged, expressing the devastation, anger, and hurt befalling them. With each subsequent phone call, Paul began to bear some of the burden that his past colleagues were bearing. He could feel his neck and back grow tense, he started to have difficulty sleeping, and he was feeling a churning in his stomach during and after each phone call. After a couple of dozen contacts from his past colleagues and friends, he had to put a firm boundary in place. While he cared for his friends, it was not fair to his wife, kids, and current employer to be distracted, worried, or anxious each time a call came in. The conversations stirred up his own memories and emotions associated with his past employer. Eventually the calls and texts came to an end, and Paul—while genuinely concerned for his past colleagues and friends—was grateful to once again have this behind him.

Paul pondered—often on his drive to and from work—about the drastic fall of his former employer. His mind drifted ultimately to leadership—and its importance. The words "leader" and "leadership" are ubiquitous in today's business and organizational world. It seems there is a constant stream of new books written each year on the importance of good leadership or building good leaders. *I wonder if there has ever been a book written on actual case studies of businesses, contrasting the differences between healthy, flourishing leaders and unhealthy, toxic leaders?* Paul thought. He thought about how the meteoric fall of Strategic Solutions could be directly attributed to one word: leadership. Furthermore, the fall could be even more narrowly confined to one team: the new CEO and his cronies. While the buck ultimately stopped with the CEO, and he had to accept responsibility and deal with the consequences, the other C-suite leaders' hands were not clean. They had helped enable the CEO's questionable behaviors by not challenging or questioning him. Paul recalled that as he had contemplated the barriers in the *diminishing* level in Global's field manual, he had noted that whenever negative attitudes or behaviors contrary to the desired culture are tolerated and not confronted, they are actually endorsed and blessed. *Therefore*, Paul thought, *if the team members had awareness of the CEO's nefarious conduct and did nothing, they should also share in the consequences—legal, financial, and reputational—that follow.*

Paul's thoughts continued to race. The cost of poor leadership, selfish leaders, narcissistic leaders—it was too much to even think about. The devastation. The lives affected. The anxiety, the worry, the anger, and the bewilderment caused. So many people now out of work worrying over how to pay their mortgages or rent, how to put food on their tables, how to put fuel in their vehicles. All through no fault of their own. Paul shook his head. *I must stop thinking about this*, he thought. *I have to stop worrying. I made the decision to leave that place, and in the past is where I need to leave it.*

As Paul finished his last thought, he was pulling into the parking lot of his office. He parked, he paused, and he prayed. "God, thank you so much for bringing me to Global. Thank you for Jude and his leadership. He isn't perfect, you know, Lord," he said with a chuckle, "but I am so grateful he is humble, he expresses empathy, he empowers his team, and he has an unwavering commitment to excellence. More importantly, he loves You and he is my friend." After praying, Paul went inside, walked down the hallway to Jude's office, and gave him the biggest bear hug. "Thank you for being my friend and my leader, and for being you, Jude," he said. "I love you, man!"

GRATITUDE

For years, I dreamed of writing a book. Never in my wildest imagination did I envision writing a second book within a year of my first book, *unSatisfied: When Less Is More,* being released. To compare the writing experience between *unSatisfied* and *unEngaged* would be like trying to compare experiencing the Indianapolis 500 and watching paint dry. The former describes my experience this time around; the latter, my experience the first time. Okay, maybe that comparison is a little dramatic, but here is my point: with the first book, I had no idea what I was doing, and I didn't know what I didn't know. My unknowns turned out to be much, *much* greater than I could have imagined. The experience of writing this book was pleasant, fun, and a great adventure. Don't get me wrong; it was still a hell of a lot of work. However, because of what I learned the first time around, this experience was so much different.

Not only was the writing of this book a completely different experience, but so was the publishing.

In the middle of the process, I had to change horses. While dismounting from one and finding another, I was in a tumultuous and unknown season of not knowing how—or even if—this book would get published. Nicole Jobe, my editor, introduced me to Kat Dixon, and then Ballast Books became my new partner and publisher for this book—and hopefully others forthcoming. Kat, thank you! You are amazing to work with, and I am so grateful for you and the Ballast Books team.

Nicole also introduced me to Tara Taylor, who did a masterful job with the proofreading phase. The Lord knows that my brain gets ahead of my fingers sometimes, but with Tara's skillful eye, those errors are no match for her.

My personal board of directors. My wife, Tiffani, Garrett ("Gary") Cooper, Scott Pflughoeft, and Chuck Yeager, thank you! Your encouragement, challenge, grace, and confrontation have made me better. You are "iron sharpening iron" to me. Without you, I would have veered off this path or abandoned the journey. I love you each individually and collectively. Thank you from the bottom of my heart.

Friends. I am truly blessed with the love, belief, and support of some amazing people. Mike Kooistra, you squeeze a buffalo nickel until it pisses—and I love that about you, man. I am grateful for that first breakfast together at Bob Evans over twenty-three years ago. What an adventure it has been! I look forward to the next twenty-three years. Scott Pflughoeft, our "decompression time" that almost always includes some kind of "brown water" is something I treasure and look forward to. Thank you for doing life with me. Verlin and Pat Rice, thank you for your love, support, and encouragement; thank you even more for sharing your lives with me and allowing me to be me, even though I think Verlin wishes there would be less of that sometimes. Gabe Clark, you inspire me! Keep pressing on and leaning into who God has made you to be. BG Allen, thinking, discussing, and dreaming with you is something I look forward to every time we talk. Thank you for being my friend. Bill and Sue Lyne, thank you for your love and support for over thirty years. I love you both dearly! Dr. John Lovell, thank you for your friendship and coaching over the years; I love learning from you. Derek Dall'Olmo, thank you for believing in me, and thank you, more importantly, for being my friend. Derek Laliberte, you inspire me! Ted Thompson, thank you, my friend, for your faithful prayers every week; I appreciate you so very much.

Kate Volman. Your coaching and encouragement helped get me to the finish line of the first book, and now look what happened: a second one! Thank you for investing in me, and thank you for writing the Foreword of this book. I am grateful for you, your support, and your friendship.

Todd Mason. Thanks for allowing me to share your story in this book; more importantly, thank you for being my friend.

Nicole Jobe. Thank you for your guidance and coaching, and for using the amazing gifts that God has given you to support me and this book. Your coaching, feedback, and training during the writing process of the first book were the defining reasons the experiences between the first book and second book were so vastly different. Thank you for believing in me! You not only used your gifts of content and line editing for this book, but you opened your network to help me find a proofreader and a new publishing partner. Thank you so very much for helping get this book to the finish line when everything became unknown in the middle of the process. I appreciate you more than words can describe!

Michael Fox. Thank you for being my friend and spiritual director. Thank you for jumping in when I needed help with the cover design. I appreciate you!

Gunnar Rogers. I deeply appreciate your help with PR, marketing, website development, blog editing, newsletter launch, and much more. However, and more importantly, your belief in me, encouragement, and support has been more than I could ever ask for. My dear friend and colleague, I would not want to be on this journey without you!

My Kids. Quentin, Danielle, and Blake, being your dad has been one of the most precious and important things I get to do in this life. You have blessed me, you have challenged me, and you have inspired me. My prayer for each of you is that God blesses each of you greatly, that you live fully integrated lives that are flourishing, and that you live each day reflecting Jesus wherever you work, live, play, and worship.

As in the Gratitude of my first book, a special thank you to Scotty "the Dood," the family's hyperactive, hyperloving goldendoodle with separation anxiety—my typing companion who kept me company on those cool evenings outside. He hates the smell of cigar and curls his lip every time he catches a whiff, but he didn't leave my side.

My Bride. To my beautiful bride since November 1996, Tiffani. I am rarely at a loss for words, but "thank you" seems too hollow, too little. Your love, encouragement, and belief in me is too much for me to comprehend. You believed in me long before I believed in myself, and you still do. You make me a better husband, dad, and man. I love you!

My Savior, Jesus. Hallowed is Your name. Your Kingdom come; Your will be done. You have demonstrated your *chesed* to me time and again. I am grateful, humbled, and blessed beyond what I could ever ask or imagine. Thank You.

May everyone who reads these words intentionally choose to pursue a flourishing life with empathy, empowerment, and excellence as the foundation for who you are and whatever you do. May it be so!

AUTHOR BIO

Matt Lesser started his career leading his family's struggling business. It quickly failed, and Matt experienced a suicidal depression. Out of the ashes, a new business emerged and grew from three people to nearly two hundred while experiencing a twenty-fold increase in revenue. Matt served in C-Suite roles in private equity, banking, and commercial uniforms before founding Uniquely Normal, LLC, to help leaders build flourishing organizations. Matt is the bestselling author of *unSatisfied: When Less is More* and has spoken to and facilitated rooms packed with leaders around the world for now more than twenty years. Matt lives in northeast Indiana with his family.